PLEASE
STOP
HELPING
US

PLEASE STOP HELPING US

How Liberals
Make It Harder
for Blacks to Succeed

JASON L. RILEY

Encounter Books
New York • London

First American edition published in 2014 by Encounter Books,
an activity of Encounter for Culture and Education, Inc.,
a nonprofit, tax exempt corporation.
Encounter Books website address: www.encounterbooks.com

Manufactured in the United States and printed on
acid-free paper. The paper used in this publication meets
the minimum requirements of ANSI/NISO Z39.48 1992
(R 1997) (*Permanence of Paper*).

FIRST AMERICAN EDITION

LIBRARY OF CONGRESS CATALOGING-IN-PUBLICATION DATA
Riley, Jason (Jason L.)
Please stop helping us: how liberals make it harder for blacks to succeed/
Jason L. Riley.
pages cm
Includes bibliographical references and index.
ISBN 978-1-59403-725-2 (hardback)—ISBN 978-1-59403-726-9 (ebook)
1. African Americans—Government policy. 2. African Americans—Social
conditions—21st century. 3. African Americans—Economic conditions—
21st century. 4. United States—Social policy. 5. Liberalism—United States.
6. Social mobility—United States. I. Title.
E185.86.R55 2014
305.896'073—dc23

2013046338

To Shelby Steele and Thomas Sowell,
for their inspiration and friendship

CONTENTS

INTRODUCTION

It has been nearly half a century since President Lyndon Johnson's 1965 commencement address at Howard University, the historically black college in Washington, D.C. He had signed the Civil Rights Act a year earlier and would sign the Voting Rights Act just two months later. But Johnson's speech wasn't a victory lap, as some anticipated. Instead, it was mainly about what government should do next on behalf of blacks. This was merely the "end of the beginning," he said, quoting Winston Churchill.

"That beginning is freedom; and the barriers to that freedom are tumbling down. Freedom is the right to share, share fully and equally, in American society—to vote, to hold a job, to enter a public place, to go to school," said Johnson. "But freedom is not enough. You do not wipe away the scars of centuries by saying: 'Now you are free to go where you want and do as you desire, and choose the leaders you please.'

"You do not take a person who, for years, has been hobbled by chains and liberate him, bring him up to the starting line of a race and then say, 'you are free to compete with all the others,' and still justly believe that you have been completely fair."

Johnson said that the "next and the more profound stage of the battle for civil rights" was "not just freedom but opportunity" and "not just equality as a right and a theory but equality as a fact and equality as a result."

The president's speech "hushed the crowd" of five thousand, wrote historian Taylor Branch. "The June 4 address soon would tear the historical sky like a lightning bolt." At the time, the country was more focused on the war in Vietnam, but Johnson had launched another war at home. It was a war on poverty and racial inequality, and he was going to win it by redistributing wealth and pushing numbers-based racial remedies.

"An almost bewildering array of Great Society programs was launched, all with the central purpose of transferring tax dollars from the middle- and high-income classes to the low-income class," wrote Stanford economist Martin Anderson. "Millions of government checks, for tens of billions of dollars, were printed and mailed and cashed. The most ambitious attempt to redistribute income ever undertaken in the United States had begun."

These were heady days for Democrats, of course. "Johnson had just been elected in a landslide over Barry Goldwater," noted a 1985 *New York Times* article commemorating the twentieth anniversary of the Great Society. "For the only time in this century except for four years in the late 1930's, a President's party had a 2-to-1 majority in both houses of Congress. The economy was strong and growing. And most people not only shared the President's dream for an end to poverty and racial injustice and a better life for all Americans but also believed with him that it was in the Government's power to fulfill that dream."

But what if Johnson was mistaken? What if there are limits to what government can do beyond removing barriers to freedom? What if the best that we can hope for from our elected officials are policies that promote equal opportunity? What if public-policy makers risk creating more barriers to progress when the goal is the ever-elusive "equality as a result"? At what point does the helping start hurting?

This book examines the track record of the political left's serial altruism over the past half century. Have popular government policies and programs that are aimed at helping blacks worked as intended? And where black advancement has occurred, do these government efforts deserve the credit that they so often receive? The intentions behind welfare programs, for example, may be noble. But in practice they have slowed the self-development that proved necessary for other groups to advance. Minimum-wage laws might lift earnings for people who are already employed, but they also have a long history of pricing blacks out of the labor force. Affirmative action in higher education was intended to address past discrimination, but the result is fewer black college graduates—particularly in the fields of math and science—than we'd have in the absence of racial preferences. And so it goes, with everything from soft-on-crime laws that make black neighborhoods more dangerous to policies that limit school choice out of a mistaken belief that charter schools and voucher programs harm the traditional public schools that most low-income students attend.

In theory these efforts are meant to help. In practice they become barriers to moving forward. *Please Stop Helping Us* lays bare these counterproductive results. People of goodwill want to see more black socioeconomic advancement, but time and again the empirical data show that current methods and approaches have come up short. Upward mobility depends on work and family. Social programs that undermine the work ethic and displace fathers keep poor people poor, and perverse incentives put in place by people trying to help are manifested in black attitudes, habits, and skills. Why study hard in school if you will be held to lower academic standards? Why change antisocial behavior when people are willing to reward it, make excuses for it, or even change the law to accommodate it?

Yes, the Obama presidency is evidence that blacks have progressed politically. But if the rise of other groups is any indication, black social and economic problems are less about politics than they are about culture. The persistently high black jobless rate is more a consequence of unemployability than of discrimination in hiring. The black-white learning gap stems from a dearth of education choices for ghetto kids, not biased tests or a shortage of education funding. And although black civil rights leaders like to point to a supposedly racist criminal justice system to explain why our prisons house so many black men, it's been obvious for decades that the real culprit is black behavior—behavior too often celebrated in black culture.

In April 1865, one hundred years before Johnson addressed Howard University graduates, the abolitionist Frederick Douglass spoke at a Boston gathering of the Massachusetts Anti-Slavery Society on a similar theme. "Everybody has asked the question, and they learned to ask it early of the abolitionists, 'What should we do with the Negro?'" said Douglass. "I have had but one answer from the beginning. Do nothing with us! Your doing with us has already played the mischief with us. Do nothing with us! If the apples will not remain on the tree of their own strength, if they are worm-eaten at the core, if they are early ripe and disposed to fall, let them fall.... And if the Negro cannot stand on his own legs, let him fall also. All I ask is, give him a chance to stand on his own legs!"

Douglass was stressing the primacy of group self-development, a not uncommon sentiment among black elites in the decades following the Civil War. Booker T. Washington, who like Douglass was born a slave, said that "It is important and right that all privileges of the law be ours, but it is vastly more important that we be prepared for the exercise of these privileges." Douglass and Washington didn't downplay the need for the government to secure equal rights for blacks, and both were optimistic that it would happen eventually. But both men also understood the limits of government benevolence. Blacks would have to ready *themselves* to meet the far bigger challenge of being in a position to take advantage of opportunities, once equal rights had been secured. The history of 1960s liberal social policies is largely a history of ignoring this wisdom. There is no question that the civil rights lobby has benefited tremendously from the programs launched by the Great Society. So has a Democratic Party that rewards black constituents with government handouts. The following pages discuss whether the folks whom these groups claim to represent are better off than they otherwise would be.

01

BLACK MAN
IN THE
WHITE HOUSE

In the fall of 2011, nearly three years after Barack Obama won the keys to the White House, the president's job-approval rating had slipped below 50 percent for the first time. No one wondered why. The official unemployment rate stood at 9 percent; economic growth was stagnant; and survey after survey demonstrated that Americans, a normally optimistic bunch, had become increasingly pessimistic about the country's future. One clear exception was black Americans, who of course had overwhelmingly supported Obama's historic election. Polls showed that white support for the president fell by 25 percentage points between his inauguration in January 2009 and September 2011, when it rested at just 33 percent. Yet even as the country endured the worst economic downturn in generations, black fealty toward Obama remained largely undiminished.

This exception was notable because the downturn hit blacks especially hard. In September 2011 white unemployment was 8 percent, versus a black unemployment rate of 16 percent. For black men it was 18 percent, and for black teens the jobless rate topped 44 percent. Nor was employment the only area where blacks as a group had regressed economically under Obama. According to the Census Bureau, black homeownership rates in 2011 had fallen to a point where the black-white gap was the widest since 1960, wiping out more than four decades of black gains.

Traditionally, homeownership has been a measure of economic well-being, and home equity is a major source of collateral for people seeking bank loans to start a business. Aside from the financial benefits, studies have shown that the children of homeowners tend to perform better in school and have fewer behavioral problems—outcomes of particular relevance to the disproportionate number of black communities where school completion rates are low and crime rates are high.

Despite this grim economic picture, blacks backed Obama in the third year of his presidency almost as strongly as they had on Election Day. Historically speaking, it fit a pattern. Between 1980 and 2004 black support for the Democratic presidential candidate ranged between 83 and 90 percent. Yet Barack Obama managed to squeeze even more out of this voting bloc. He won 95 percent of the black vote in 2008, a year that also saw a record percentage of eligible black voters turn out to elect the nation's first black president. The surge was driven mostly by black women and younger voters; white voter turnout in 2008 actually fell from what it had been four years earlier. And while black support for Obama had declined slightly by the fall of 2011, it seemed unlikely that black America would be abandoning the president in significant numbers anytime soon. According to Gallup, Obama's approval rating among blacks had dipped from an average of 92 percent in 2009 to 86 percent in mid-2011. Separate polling by Pew showed that Obama's support among blacks remained essentially unchanged at 90 percent over the same period.

If anything, these polls were underestimating black support for the president. In 2012, black turnout would increase from 2008 and 93 percent would pull the lever for Obama, notwithstanding clear evidence that blacks had lost ground on his watch. When Obama took office in January 2009, unemployment was 12.7 percent for blacks and 7.1 percent for whites. On Election Day in November 2012 it was 14.3 percent for blacks and 7 percent for whites, which meant that the black-white unemployment gap had not only persisted, but widened, during Obama's first term.

It could be that blacks, like so many others who supported his reelection in 2012, were cutting the president slack because the economy was already in bad shape when Obama took office. As one black voter put it to a reporter in August 2011, "No president, not Bush, not Obama, could turn the mess that we are in around in four years." But in the past, the black approval rating of a president had tended to correlate with the jobless rate. Yet black unemployment was lower under George W. Bush than it had been at any point during the Obama administration. In addition, the black-white income disparity that widened under Obama actually narrowed in the 1980s under President Ronald Reagan, even though Reagan also inherited a weak economy from his predecessor. The Great Recession that began under George W. Bush in December 2007 had officially ended in June 2009, six months after Obama took office.

Economic historians, citing one hundred and fifty years of U.S. business cycles, generally agree that the deeper the recession, the stronger the recovery. Not so under Obama, and not so especially for blacks. A report released by two former Census Bureau officials in August 2013 found that since the end of the recession, median household incomes had fallen 3.6 percent for whites and 10.9 percent for blacks.[1] Which means that even when controlling for the effects of the economic slowdown that Obama inherited, under his presidency blacks have been worse off both in absolute terms and relative to whites. When Fox News's Sean Hannity asked black talk-show host Tavis Smiley in October of 2013 if black Americans were "better off five years into the Obama presidency," Smiley responded: "Let me answer your question very forthrightly: No, they are not. The data is going to indicate, sadly, that when the Obama administration is over, black people will have lost ground in every single leading economic indicator category. On that regard, the president ought to be held responsible."[2] Blacks seemed to disagree. According to Gallup, Obama's job-approval rating among blacks was 85 percent (versus just 43 percent among all groups) when Smiley made those remarks.

Broad racial solidarity is another possible explanation for why blacks have remained so bullish on Obama despite his economic record. A black member of Congress told political scientist Carol Swain that "one of the advantages, and disadvantages, of representing blacks is their shameless loyalty . . . You can almost get away with raping babies and be forgiven. You don't have *any* vigilance about your performance."[3]

The political left, which has long embraced identity politics, encourages racial and ethnic loyalty. It is manifest in liberal support for multiculturalism, hate-crime laws, racially gerrymandered voting districts, affirmative-action quotas, and other policies. "Stick together, black people," says popular black radio host Tom Joyner, an Obama booster. "No matter what policies he pursues, the president's racialized embodiment stands as a symbol of triumphant black achievement," asserts MSNBC's Melissa Harris-Perry.[4] Black politicians have long played off of the notion that blacks owe allegiance to "their own." Some of the group's most vicious insults— "Uncle Tom," "Oreo," "sellout"—are reserved for those deemed race traitors. Supporting Obama regardless of his job performance is therefore seen by many blacks as not only the right thing to do but the "black" thing to do.

The administration itself has stoked this sentiment in hopes of maintaining strong black support. It has pushed to loosen "racist" drug-sentencing laws. It has sued employers who use criminal background checks to screen job applicants. It has unleashed federal housing officials on white suburban residential communities that it considered insufficiently integrated. The goal is to sustain goodwill with the civil rights establishment and black voters, even if these measures are more symbolic than substantive. Black incarceration rates are not driven by drug laws; empirical research shows that employers who check criminal histories are *more likely* to hire blacks; and polls have long shown that most black people have no interest in living in mostly white neighborhoods. Yet these kinds of measures are used to foster an "us-versus-them" mentality among blacks and then exploit such thinking for partisan political gain.

Liberals like to complain that, the twice-elected President Obama notwithstanding, we are not a "post-racial" society. The reality is that they wouldn't have it any other way. Race consciousness helps cohere the political left, and black liberalism's main agenda is keeping race front and center in our national conversations. That's why, for example, much more common black-on-black crimes take a back seat to much less common white-on-black crimes. The last thing that organizations like the NAACP want is for America to get "beyond" race. In their view, racial discrimination in one form or another remains a significant barrier to black progress, and government action is the best solution.

The White House and its allies played the race card in earnest after the president kicked off his reelection campaign in 2011. U.S. Attorney General Eric Holder, in speech after speech, claimed that photo-ID voting requirements hurt minorities, even though such requirements are favored by a large majority of all voters, regardless of race.[5] "Are we willing to allow this era—our era—to be remembered as the age when our nation's proud tradition of expanding the franchise was cut short?" said Holder. "Call on all political parties . . . to resist the temptation to suppress certain votes," he added. "Keep urging policymakers at every level to reevaluate our election systems—and to reform them in ways that encourage, not limit, participation."[6]

Ben Jealous, then head of the NAACP, pressured the Obama administration to oppose these voter ID laws. He told NPR that these requirements have nothing to do with ballot integrity, as proponents insist, and are akin to Reconstruction-era poll taxes. "You look historically, you look presently, and what you see is that when our democracy expands, somebody turns around and tries to contract it," said Jealous. "You saw it after the Civil War. You see it now after the election of the first black president."[7]

Voter ID laws preceded Barack Obama's 2008 election, and in places like Georgia and Indiana minority turnout increased after the laws were passed. A 2007 study by the Heritage Foundation concluded that "in general, respondents in photo identification and non-photo identification states are *just as likely* to report voting compared to respondents from states that only required voters to state their name."[8] The findings applied to white, black, and Latino voters alike. The spectacle of a black president's black attorney general pretending that the black franchise is in jeopardy in twenty-first-century America struck many people as intellectually dishonest political pandering. That included black lawmakers who have argued that voter ID laws are necessary to help ensure ballot integrity. "When I was a congressman, I took the path of least resistance on this subject for an African American politician," wrote Artur Davis, a former member of the Congressional Black Caucus who left office in 2010. "Without any evidence to back it up, I lapsed into the rhetoric of various partisans and activists who contend that requiring photo identification to vote is a suppression tactic aimed at thwarting black voter participation. The truth is that the most aggressive contemporary voter suppression in the African American community, at least in Alabama, is the wholesale manufacture of ballots, at the polls and absentee, in parts of the Black Belt."[9]

It so happens that black voter turnout surpassed white turnout for the first time on record in 2012, even while more and more states were implementing these supposedly racist voter ID laws. "About two in three eligible blacks (66.2 percent) voted in the 2012 presidential election, higher than the 64.1 percent of non-Hispanic whites who did so," according to the Census Bureau. "Blacks were the only race or ethnic group to show a significant increase between the 2008 and 2012 elections in the likelihood of voting (from 64.7 percent to 66.2 percent)." Was this simply a case of more blacks turning out to support a black candidate? Perhaps, but as the Census Bureau notes, the trend predates the Obama presidency. "The 2012 increase in voting among blacks continues what has been a long-term trend: since 1996, turnout rates have risen 13 percentage points to the highest levels of any recent presidential election."[10] The trend was most pronounced in red states like Alabama, Kentucky, and Mississippi. Black voter turnout in 2012 surpassed white turnout by statistically significant margins in Florida, Virginia, and the Carolinas, as well as in states with the strictest voter ID laws, such as Tennessee, Georgia, and Indiana. Democrats claim such laws deny blacks the franchise, but where is the evidence?

Obama typically has employed surrogates to make blunt racial appeals—recall Vice President Joe Biden telling a mostly black audience on the 2012 campaign trail that Republicans want to "put y'all back in chains"—but the nation's first black president is not above personally using this sort of rhetoric, as he has sometimes done in response to the relatively few black critics of his presidency who have dared to go public. During Obama's first term, Democratic Representative Emanuel Cleaver of Missouri told the *Wall Street Journal* that he was "frustrated with the president" over the stratospheric black unemployment rate. The congressman said that he understood Obama's reluctance to be too closely associated with the black community and thus be seen as favoring blacks over other Americans. Nevertheless, "you would think that if any group in America had 20 percent to 25 percent unemployment, it would generate all kinds of attention," he said. "The Labor Department would understandably and necessarily begin to concentrate on what can we do to reduce this level of unemployment. Congress would give great time on the floor for debate on what can be done." After other prominent black liberals—including academic Cornel West, commentator Tavis Smiley, and Democratic Representative Maxine Waters of California—began griping about Obama's lack of attention to the economic problems of the black underclass, the president responded in a sharply worded address to the Congressional Black Caucus. "I expect all of you to march with me and press on," he said, evoking the language of Martin Luther King Jr. and other black preachers of the civil rights era. "Take off your bedroom slippers, put on your marching shoes. Shake it off. Stop complaining, stop grumbling, stop crying. We are going to press on."

But racial allegiance doesn't entirely explain black attitudes toward Obama, according to David Bositis, a political scientist at the Joint Center for Political and Economic Studies who specializes in black issues. "You have to put the choice that African Americans are making in context," he told the *Huffington Post* in 2011. "Certainly there may be some residual good feelings from that historic moment in 2008. But support for the president remains strong because there is no real menu of political options for African Americans."[11]

Bositis is a liberal who holds conservatives in low regard, but he is correct in noting that GOP outreach to blacks in recent decades has ranged somewhere between inadequate and nonexistent. In the main, black voters don't choose between Democratic and Republican candidates; they vote Democrat or they stay home. Many liberals are quick to assume that racial animus explains the lack of any serious GOP effort to woo blacks. But in his memoir, Supreme Court Justice Clarence Thomas offered an alternative explanation: political pragmatism. Recounting his days as head of the Equal Employment Opportunity Commission under President Reagan in the early 1980s, Thomas wrote that his "main quarrel" with the Reagan administration was that he thought it needed a positive civil rights agenda, instead of merely railing against racial preferences. "But I found it impossible to get the administration to pay attention to such matters," he wrote.

> *Too many of the president's political appointees seemed more interested in playing to the conservative bleachers—and I'd come to realize, as I told a reporter, that "conservatives don't exactly break their necks to tell blacks that they're welcome."*

Thomas next offered a theory as to why that was the case:

> *Was it because they were prejudiced? Perhaps some of them were, but the real reason, I suspected, was that blacks didn't vote for Republicans, nor would Democrats work with President Reagan on civil-rights issues. As a result there was little interest within the administration in helping a constituency that wouldn't do anything in return to help the president.*
>
> *My suspicions were confirmed when I offered my assistance to President Reagan's reelection campaign, only to be met with near-total indifference. One political consultant was honest enough to tell me straight out that since the president's reelection strategy didn't include the black vote, there was no role for me.*[12]

Prior to Obama's win in 2008, the GOP had won five out of seven presidential elections. Over that same stretch, fewer than 10 percent of blacks typically identified as Republicans. Black voters today remain nonessential to GOP electoral success, and time spent courting one group leaves less time to court others who are deemed key to winning. When this dynamic changes—

when GOP candidates begin to think that they need black voters to prevail—perhaps we will see a more sustained effort to win over blacks. In recent years, the GOP has been having a spirited intraparty debate over whether it can continue to win elections without more Hispanic voters, given the rapid growth of the Latino population. Republicans haven't been paying half as much attention to blacks. This reality obviously has allowed Democrats to take the black vote for granted, and Barack Obama is no exception. But it has also resulted in a state of affairs that is arguably even more pernicious. To wit: Many blacks, at the urging of civil rights leaders and the liberal intelligentsia who share the Democratic Party's big-government agenda, place a premium on the political advancement of the race. Whether political power is in fact a necessary precondition for group advancement is rarely questioned. It's simply assumed to be true.

"What began as a protest movement is being challenged to translate itself into a political movement," wrote Bayard Rustin in a 1965 essay, "From Protest to Politics: The Future of the Civil Rights Movement." Rustin, chief organizer of the 1963 March on Washington, wrote that "More than voter registration is involved here. A conscious bid for *political power* is being made."[13] (Here and throughout this book, emphases in excerpted matter are from the original.) In his 1967 book, *Where Do We Go From Here: Chaos or Community?*, Martin Luther King Jr. wrote, "How shall we make every house worker and every laborer a demonstrator, a voter, a canvasser and a student?" James Farmer, another prominent member of the civil rights old guard, also envisioned political power as the way forward for blacks. "We can no longer rely on pressuring and cajoling political units toward desired actions," he wrote in 1965. "We must be in a position of power, a position to change these political units when they are not responsive. The only way to achieve political objectives is through power, political power."[14]

By and large, black intellectuals today have not changed their thinking in this regard. "Black politics—African Americans' ability to mobilize, influence policy, demand accountability from government officials, and contribute and influence American political discourse, all in the service of black interests—is still extremely weak," wrote Michael Dawson, a professor of political science at the University of Chicago. For the professor—and his view is quite typical on the left—black political progress is essential to black socioeconomic progress. "Racial inequality remains a brute fact of life in this country," he wrote. "In order to transform America into a just democracy, it is necessary to rebuild black politics."[15]

For more than a century black leaders have tangled with one another over whether to pursue economic independence or focus their energies on integrating political, corporate, and educational institutions. W. E. B. Du Bois, author of the groundbreaking 1903 treatise *The Souls of Black Folk*, argued for the latter, while his contemporary, Booker T. Washington, said "political activity alone" is not the answer. In addition, wrote Washington, "you must have property, industry, skill, economy, intelligence and character." Where Washington wanted to focus on self-determination through independent black schools and businesses, Du Bois argued that civil rights are more important because political power is necessary to protect any economic gains. Much has been made of this rivalry—maybe too much. What matters most is that the two men differed mainly in emphasis, not objectives. Washington never renounced equal rights, and Du Bois acknowledged the need for vocational education as a means to self-improvement.

Washington inherited the mantle of black leadership from the abolitionist Frederick Douglass, who gained fame through his slave memoirs and oratory and ultimately helped persuade President Lincoln to sign the Emancipation Proclamation. In 1881 Washington founded Alabama's Tuskegee Institute, which trained recently freed slaves to become teachers. He became a national figure in 1895 after giving a speech in Atlanta in which he called for racial conciliation and urged blacks to focus on economic self-advancement. For the next two decades Washington would be America's preeminent black leader. He advised presidents, and wrote an autobiography that was translated into seven languages and became the best-selling book ever written by someone black. Andrew Carnegie called him the second father of the country. John D. Rockefeller and J. P. Morgan were major benefactors. Harvard and Dartmouth gave him honorary degrees. Mark Twain was an admirer.

After the NAACP was established in 1909, and as Du Bois's prominence grew, Washington's power base weakened. But even after his death in 1915, Washington remained widely appreciated within the black community and elsewhere. Schools and parks were named in his honor. His likeness appeared on a U.S. postage stamp. In 1942 a Liberty ship was christened the Booker T. Washington. And in 1956, marking the one-hundredth anniversary of Washington's birth, President Dwight Eisenhower created a national monument to the former slave.

But Washington's legacy would come under assault in the 1960s, when civil rights advocates turned in earnest to protest politics. Washington had stressed self-improvement, not immediate political rights through confrontation. The new black leaders dismissed such methods, along with the man best known for utilizing them. Du Bois's vision, by way of the NAACP, Malcolm X, and Martin Luther King Jr., had prevailed. By the 1960s, "blacks throughout the United States increasingly condemned [Washington] as having acquiesced in the racial discrimination that so many were now challenging in restaurants, waiting rooms, and courthouses," wrote Washington biographer Robert Norrell.[16] John Lewis, the 1960s civil rights activist who would later become a congressman, suggested that Washington deserved to be "ridiculed and vilified by his own people for working so closely with white America."

The black left today continues to view Washington not as a pragmatist, but as someone who naively accommodated white racism. "This distortion of Washington contributed to a narrowing of the limits Americans have put on black aspirations and accomplishments," wrote Norrell. "After the 1960s, any understanding of the role of black leaders was cast in the context of Martin Luther King Jr.'s leadership, with the implication that African Americans can rise in American life only through direct-action protests against the political order."[17] Not only has Washington's legacy thus been maligned, but several generations of blacks have come to believe that the only legitimate means of group progress is political agitation of the NAACP-Jesse Jackson-Al Sharpton variety. If you are more interested in black self-development than in keeping whites on the defensive, you're accommodating racism.

In a January 2014 interview with the *New Yorker* magazine, Obama invoked Washington's name unfavorably to push back at liberal black critics who accused the president of being insufficiently concerned with white racism. "There have been times where some thoughtful and sometimes not so thoughtful African-American commentators have gotten on both Michelle and me, suggesting that we are not addressing enough sort of institutional barriers and racism, and we're engaging in sort of up-by-the-bootstraps, Booker T. Washington messages that let the larger society off the hook," said Obama.[18]

"Washington's style of interracial engagement has been all but forgotten, and when remembered, usually disparaged: he put a premium on finding consensus and empathizing with other groups, and by his example encouraged dominant groups to do the same," wrote Norrell. "He cautioned that when people protest constantly about their mistreatment, they soon get a reputation as complainers, and others stop listening to their grievances. Blacks needed a reputation for being hard-working, intelligent, and patriotic, Washington taught, and not for being aggrieved."[19]

Were Du Bois and King alive today, they would no doubt be glad to know that between 1970 and 2001 the number of black elected officials in the United States grew from fewer than fifteen hundred to more than nine thousand. But they would also have to acknowledge that this political success had not redounded to the black underclass. Between 1940 and 1960—that is, before the major civil rights victories, and at a time when black political power was nearly nonexistent—the black poverty rate fell from 87 percent to 47 percent. Yet between 1972 and 2011—that is, after major civil rights gains, as well as the implementation of Great Society programs—it barely declined, from 32 percent to 28 percent, and remained three times the white rate, which is about what it was in 1972.[20] By 2013 Mississippi had more black elected officials than any other state, but it also continues to have one of the highest black poverty rates in the nation.

Other measures of black well-being also don't seem to have improved along with black political progress over the decades. Impressive socioeconomic advancement has been made and the black middle class has grown, but wide black-white gaps remain, not only with regard to income but also respecting educational achievement, labor-force participation, incarceration rates, and other measures. While blacks were steadily increasing their numbers in Congress and among elected officials at the state and local levels in the 1970s, '80s, and '90s, black welfare dependency rose, as did black teen unemployment, black crime, and black births to single mothers.

The economist Thomas Sowell has spent decades researching racial and ethnic groups in the United States and internationally. And his findings show that political activity generally has not been a factor in the rise of groups from poverty to prosperity. Many Germans came to the United States as indentured servants during colonial times, and while working to pay off the cost of the voyage they shunned politics. Only after they had risen economically did Germans begin seeking public office, culminating with the elections of Presidents Hoover and Eisenhower. Today Asian Americans are the nation's best-educated and highest-earning racial group. A 2013 Pew study reported that 49 percent of Asians age 25 and older hold bachelor's degrees, versus 31 percent of whites and 18 percent of blacks. The median household income for Asians is $66,000, which is $12,000 more than white households and double that of black households. Yet Asians have little political clout in the United States. There have been a handful of prominent Asian American politicians, like Governors Bobby Jindal of Louisiana and Nikki Haley of South Carolina, but Asians have tended to avoid politics, compared with other groups. Between 1990 and 2000 the number of elected officials grew by 23 percent among blacks but only by 4 percent among Asians. Even Asian voter participation lags behind other groups; in 2008, Asians were significantly less likely than both blacks and whites to have voted. A similar pattern can be found among Chinese populations in southeast Asia and the Caribbean, the English in Argentina, Italians in the United States, and Jews in Britain. In each case, economic gains have generally preceded political gains. "Empirically, political activity and political success have been neither necessary nor sufficient for economic advancement," wrote Sowell. "Nor has eager political participation or outstanding success in politics been translated into faster group achievement."[21]

Moreover, in those instances where the political success of a minority group has come first, the result has often been *slower* socioeconomic progress. The Irish immigrants who came to the United States in the mid-nineteenth century arrived from a country where 80 percent of the population was rural. Yet they settled in industrial centers like New York, Philadelphia, and Boston and took low-skill jobs. Their rise from poverty was especially slow—as late as 1920, 80 percent of all Irish women working in America were domestic servants—despite the fact that Irish-run political organizations dominated local government in several big cities with large Irish populations. "To most Americans today, it is not immediately obvious that the black migrants who left the rural South for the industrial cities of the North starting in the 1940s resemble the Irish immigrants who left rural Ireland and crossed the ocean to the great cities of the Atlantic seaboard starting in the 1840s," wrote political historian Michael Barone. "Yet the resemblances are many."[22] Among other things, explained Barone,

> both groups looked to control of government as a means of advancement, and both excelled at politics. They built their own political organizations, modeled on their churches: the Irish, hierarchical political machines; blacks, ad hoc organizations assembled by charismatic local leaders. They were initially the object of competition between Democrats and Whigs or Republicans, but within about twenty years both became heavily, almost unanimously, Democratic. Both used politics to create large numbers of public sector jobs for their own people. In some cities where they were majorities—Boston and Jersey

City for the Irish, Detroit and Washington for blacks—they created predatory politics, which overloaded the public payroll and neglected to enforce the law, ultimately damaging the cities' private economies.[23]

Yet it was only after the decline of the famed Irish political machines that average Irish incomes began to rise. Irish patronage politics was not the deciding factor in group advancement, Barone noted.

Society addressed the ills of the Irish through private charities, the settlement house movement, temperance societies, and police forces, all of which tried to improve individuals' conduct and to help people conform to the standards of the larger society. The Irish rose to average levels of income and education by the 1950s, and in 1960 an Irish Catholic was elected president of the United States.[24]

Sowell and Barone are conservatives, but some liberal scholars have made the same point. In their 1991 case study of Atlanta, political scientist Gary Orfield and coauthor Carole Ashkinaze described the city as "a center of black power" that at the time had been run by "two nationally prominent black mayors" for more than a decade. "Atlanta has been celebrated as a black Mecca, where the doors are open and a critical mass of black leadership already exists," they wrote. "Atlanta's first black mayor, Maynard Jackson"—elected to the first of his three terms in 1973—"expressed this in his frequent public promises to give minorities 'a piece of the pie.'" Jackson and his successor, Andrew Young, implemented racial preference programs for hiring city workers and contractors, and the number of successful black firms increased rapidly. But according to Orfield and Ashkinaze, average blacks in Atlanta were left behind, and the black underclass lost ground.

"If economic growth and black political leadership were sufficient to resolve racial differences in the 1980s, tremendous mobility for the region's poor blacks should have taken place," they wrote. "Indeed, some blacks made it. On average, however, the situation of the black population relative to whites became significantly worse in very important respects." The authors went on to make a broader point about intentions versus results. "The late 1960s' prophecies of dangerous racial separation have given way to a vague hope that racial inequalities are being resolved, perhaps through the election of black officials," wrote Orfield and Ashkinaze. "Many blacks have reached positions of local power, such as mayor, county commission chairman or superintendent of schools, positions undreamed of 30 years ago. But these achievements do not necessarily produce success for blacks as a whole. In fact, they may contribute to our lack of knowledge about low-income blacks. Black officials, like their white predecessors, tend to publicize successes, not problems."[25] History, in other words, provides little indication, let alone assurance, that political success is a prerequisite of upward mobility.

The 1965 Voting Rights Act was passed to ensure black access to the ballot, particularly in the states of the Old Confederacy where blacks risked life and limb to exercise their basic rights. Vernon Jordan, a former head of the National Urban League, called it "probably the most significant accomplishment" of the civil rights movement. The right to vote is a cornerstone of our democracy, but it was routinely denied to blacks in the states where most of them lived. "Prior to the Voting Rights Act of 1965, blacks were roughly one-tenth of the Deep South's registered voters," explained J. Harvie Wilkinson in his civil rights history, *From Brown to Bakke*. "By 1970 they comprised approximately 30 percent of the Mississippi electorate, a quarter of that in South Carolina, a fifth in Alabama, Georgia, Louisiana."[26] In 1964, black voter registration in Mississippi was under 7 percent, the lowest in the region. A year after the act passed, black voter registration in Mississippi had climbed to about 60 percent, the highest in the South. The law was a success.

"Nothing short of radical federal intervention would have enfranchised southern blacks," wrote voting-rights scholar Abigail Thernstrom. "Sometimes good legislation works precisely as initially intended."[27] But like so much civil rights legislation, the law's justification soon shifted from equal opportunity to equal results. Section 5 of the Voting Rights Act requires states with a history of racially motivated voter intimidation to have any changes in voting procedures cleared by a federal court or the Justice Department. This so-called preclearance provision, always intended to be temporary, was slated to sunset after five years, but Congress renewed the provision repeatedly well after it became obvious that ballot access was no longer a problem for blacks. In 1982 a permanent part of the law, Section 2, was amended to allow for racial gerrymandering, or the drawing of voting districts to ensure that a candidate of a particular race is elected. The measure of success was no longer whether blacks had ballot access. Instead, it was whether enough black officials were being elected to office, and liberals became hell-bent on using Sections 2 and 5 to achieve proportional racial representation. "In 1965, the Voting Rights Act had been simple, transparent and elegant. Its aim was to secure basic Fifteenth Amendment rights in a region where they had been egregiously denied," wrote Thernstrom. "But the cumulative effect of these amendments was to turn the law into a constitutionally problematic, unprecedented attempt to impose what voting rights activists, along with their allies in Congress, the Justice Department, and the judiciary, viewed as a racially fair distribution of political power."[28] In 2006, Congress renewed Section 5 for another twenty-five years.

We are in the second decade of the twenty-first century, and a black man has twice been elected president in a country where blacks are only 13 percent of the population. Yet liberals continue to pretend that it's still 1965, and that voters must be segregated in order for blacks to win office. Never mind that in 1982 five black candidates from majority-white districts won seats in the North Carolina State House of Representatives. Or that from 1983 to 1995 a majority-white district in Missouri was represented in Congress by Alan Wheat, a black Democrat. Or that between 1991 and 1997 Gary Franks, a black Republican from Connecticut, represented a congressional district that was 88 percent white. Or that in 1996 Sanford Bishop, a black Democrat from Georgia, easily won reelection to Congress in a district that was only 35 percent black. Or that in 2010 Tim Scott of South Carolina and Allen West of Florida, both black Republicans, were elected to Congress from districts that are overwhelmingly white. Or that Representatives Emanuel Cleaver of Missouri and Keith Ellison of Minnesota are black Democrats who represent districts that are more than 60 percent white.

In 2008 Obama not only won the presidency of a majority-white country; he did better among white voters in Georgia, North Carolina, South Carolina, Texas, and Virginia than John Kerry in 2004 and Al Gore in 2000. Yet after the Supreme Court, in its 2013 decision *Shelby County v. Holder*, effectively nullified Section 5's "preclearance" provisions by ruling that Congress was using an outdated formula to determine which states must have federal oversight of their voting laws, Obama said he was "deeply disappointed," and complained that the ruling "upsets decades of well-established practices that help make sure voting is fair, especially in places where voting discrimination has been historically prevalent." The president and others on the left wanted the court to ignore the fact that, as Chief Justice John Roberts phrased it in his majority opinion, "history did not end in 1965." Roberts took Congress to task for pretending that nothing had changed in nearly half a century, writing:

> By the time the [Voting Rights Act of 1965] was reauthorized in 2006, there had been 40 more years of it. In assessing the "current need" for a preclearance system that treats States differently from one another today, that history cannot be ignored. During that time, largely because of the Voting Rights Act, voting tests were abolished, disparities in voter registration and turnout due to race were erased, and African-Americans attained political office in record numbers. And yet the coverage formula that Congress reauthorized in 2006 ignores these developments, keeping the focus on decades-old data relevant to decades-old problems, rather than current data reflecting current needs.

What do the current data show? Among other things, the statistics reveal that black voter registration is higher in the South than it is in other regions of the country. They show that the racial gap in voter registration and turnout is lower in the states originally covered under Section 5 than it is nationwide. Finally, they show that black turnout now exceeds white turnout in five of those six states, and that in the sixth state the disparity is less than one-half of one percent. In other words, it shows tremendous voting-rights progress.

The political left, led by Obama, played down this racial progress and expressed disappointment with the outcome of the case, but their dismay had nothing to do with any fear that black access to balloting was in jeopardy. After all, most of the Voting Rights

Act is permanent, and those who feel that a voting procedure is racially discriminatory still have legal recourse. What really concerns liberals is that the ruling could make it more difficult for them to use the Voting Rights Act to guarantee certain election results. As Roger Clegg and Joshua Thompson, who filed an amicus brief in *Shelby County v. Holder*, explained, "the principal use that federal civil-rights officials now make of Section 5 is to require racially gerrymandered and racially segregated voting districts." The argument is that racial minorities are entitled to a proportionate number of voting districts in which they are the majority. "Think about how far from the ideals of the civil-rights movement the Left's definition of civil rights has led us," wrote Clegg and Thompson. "Universities must be able to discriminate against students on the basis of skin color, and voters must be required to vote only among those of their own kind."[29]

The irony is that these efforts to go beyond the original intent of the Voting Rights Act in the name of helping blacks politically have almost certainly hampered blacks politically by limiting their appeal to nonblack voters. By creating "safe" black districts, racial gerrymandering has facilitated racial polarization and hyperpartisanship. Minority candidates have less incentive to make appeals to people outside of their racial or ethnic voting base, so winning statewide becomes more difficult. Members of the Congressional Black Caucus typically have voting records that are more liberal than the average white Democrat. "Black political progress might be greater today had the race-based districting been viewed as a temporarily needed remedy for unmistakably racist voting in the region that was only reluctantly accepting blacks as American citizens," wrote Thernstrom. Instead, as a consequence of racial gerrymandering, "elections nationwide have become more or less permanently structured to discourage politically adventuresome

African American candidates who aspire to win political office in majority-white settings."[30]

One reason that returns on black political investment have been so meager is that black politicians often act in ways that benefit themselves but don't represent the concerns of most blacks. So in addition to being overly reliant on politicians, blacks typically have poor political representation. "Pollsters have long known of the remarkable gap between the leaders and the led in black America," wrote Harvard professor Henry Louis Gates Jr.

> A 1985 survey found that most blacks favored the death penalty and prayer in public schools while most black leaders opposed these things. Most blacks opposed school busing, while most black leaders favored it. Three times as many blacks opposed abortion rights as their leaders did. Indeed, on many key social issues, blacks are more conservative than whites.[31]

As more blacks have joined the American mainstream over the past half century, this disconnect between the black politicians and civil rights leadership and the people they supposedly represent has only grown. Black America "isn't just as fissured as white America; it is more so," wrote Gates.

> And the mounting intraracial disparities mean that the realities of race no longer affect all blacks in the same way. There have been perverse consequences: in part to assuage our sense of survivor's guilt, we often cloak these differences in a romantic black nationalism—something that has become the veritable socialism of the black bourgeoisie.[32]

For years, black political leaders in New York City aligned themselves with labor unions to block the construction of a Walmart in a low-income community with persistently high unemployment. According to a Marist poll taken in 2011, 69 percent of blacks in New York would welcome a Walmart in their neighborhood. Yet these black leaders put the interests of Big Labor, which doesn't like the retailer's stance toward unions, ahead of the interests of struggling black people who could use the jobs and low-priced goods. School choice is another area where black politicians continue to oppose policies overwhelmingly supported by black voters in general and the black underclass in particular. In 2012 voters in Georgia approved Amendment 1, a ballot initiative to expand school choice in the form of charter schools in a state where one-third of high-school freshmen failed to graduate in four years. Black voters were the strongest backers of the initiative, which passed 59 percent to 41 percent. "One of the most striking results of the vote on Amendment 1," wrote journalist Douglas Blackmon, "is the absolutely extraordinary level of support received from African-American voters." The measure was supported by 61 percent of voters in the twenty Georgia counties where blacks are half of the population. And in the thirteen counties that comprise more than half of the state's black population, support was an even higher 62 percent. "The bottom line: Georgia's black counties overwhelmingly desire dramatic new alternatives to the conventional school systems that have failed them for more than a century," wrote Blackmon.

That level of support flatly contradicts one of the flimsiest canards used to criticize Amendment 1—and charter schools in general. That is: the idea that somehow charter schools end up hurting minority or poorer students while disproportionately

*helping white and middle class children. The actual performance
of charter schools in Georgia has always defied such claims.
African-American students and all children living in urban
areas with failed conventional public schools, like Atlanta, have
benefited far more from charters than any other groups.*[33]

Yet within a week of the amendment's passage, the Georgia Legislative Black Caucus joined a lawsuit to block expansion of charter schools in the state.[34]

Whatever else the election of Barack Obama represented—some have called it redemption, others have called it the triumph of style over substance—it was the ultimate victory for people who believe that black political gains are of utmost importance to black progress in America. C. T. Vivian, a close associate of Martin Luther King Jr., told Obama biographer David Remnick that "Martin Luther King was our prophet—in biblical terms, the prophet of our age. The politician of our age, who comes along to follow that prophet, is Barack Obama. Martin laid the moral and spiritual base for the political reality to follow." Since the assassinations of King and Robert Kennedy, wrote Remnick,

> *the liberal constituencies of America had been waiting for a
> savior figure. Barack Obama proposed himself. In the eyes
> of his supporters, he was a promise in a bleak landscape; he
> possessed an inspirational intelligence and an evident compe-
> tence . . . he was an embodiment of multi-ethnic inclusion when
> the country was becoming no longer white in its majority. This
> was the promise of his campaign, its reality or vain romance,
> depending on your view.*[35]

We'll call it vain romance. The sober truth is that the most important civil rights battles were fought and won four decades before the Obama presidency. The black underclass continues to face many challenges, but they have to do with values and habits, not oppression from a manifestly unjust society. Blacks have become their own worst enemy, and liberal leaders do not help matters by blaming self-inflicted wounds on whites or "society." The notion that racism is holding back blacks as a group, or that better black outcomes cannot be expected until racism has been vanquished, is a dodge. And encouraging blacks to look to politicians to solve their problems does them a disservice. As the next chapter explains, one lesson of the Obama presidency—maybe the most important one for blacks—is that having a black man in the Oval Office is less important than having one in the home.

02

CULTURE MATTERS

The last time I saw my father he was pulling away from the curb in front of my home in suburban New York City, where he'd spent the weekend visiting his two toddler grandchildren and taking in a Yankees game with his only son. I asked him to call me when he got back to Buffalo, the city where I was raised, and where he still lived with my older sister and her two daughters. I don't remember if he ever did, but a few days later my sister would phone to tell me that she had found him slumped over in his recliner when she arrived home from work one evening. Fourteen years after Mom had died, Dad was gone, too.

I have no recollection of my father ever living with my mother, or even much liking her. They married in 1964, had three children by 1972 (I was born in 1971), and would be divorced by the time Jimmy Carter took office. After the split they went out of their way to avoid speaking to one another, often using us children to communicate. Tell your mother this, or tell you father that, were common requests growing up as we shuttled back and forth between residences. But while their dislike of one another was palpable to us kids, it never seemed to interfere with our relationships with them. In fact, one of the few things they seemed to agree on was that the other was a good parent.

My sisters and I lived with our mother, but we had almost unlimited access to Dad, who took full advantage of his visiting privileges. The anthropologist Margaret Mead said that the ultimate test of any culture is whether it can successfully socialize men to willingly nurture their children. "Every known human society rests firmly on the learned nurturing behavior of men," she wrote. "Each new generation of young males learn the appropriate nurturing behavior and superimpose upon their biologically given maleness this learned parental role."[1] I don't know if my parents ever read Mead, but they certainly shared that sentiment.

Until the day he died my father was a constant presence in the lives of his children. Growing up, my sisters and I saw him Tuesdays, Thursdays, weekends, and holidays. My relationship with him was an especially close one that both he and my mother were keen to maintain. He checked my homework, helped me with my paper route, and spent hours at my side constructing and reconstructing my elaborate model train sets. My father and I were sports nuts. He taught me to hit, pitch, shoot, and tackle. He coached my Little League baseball teams. He had me on ice skates as soon as I could walk. We attended countless local college basketball games together, were Buffalo Bills season ticket holders, and regularly drove to Toronto to see the Yankees play the Blue Jays. None of this is especially remarkable fatherly behavior, of course, unless the father happens to be black. Fathers who live apart from their offspring are less likely to spend time with them, or contribute financially to their upbringing. My father distinguished himself by being there for us. And his behavior would become even more exceptional, statistically speaking, over time.

In 1965, when he was assistant secretary of labor for President Lyndon Johnson, Daniel Patrick Moynihan was already warning that the black family was in a state of crisis. Although nine in ten children in America lived with their biological father in 1960, some one in four black kids did not. By 2011 33 percent of children in the United States would be living with their mothers, but not their fathers. Among blacks the number would climb to 64 percent, or nearly two in three.

"Though income is the primary predictor, the lack of live-in fathers also is overwhelmingly a black problem, regardless of poverty status," reported the *Washington Times* in 2012, citing census data. "Among blacks, nearly 5 million children, or 54 percent, live with only their mother." Just 12 percent of poor black households have two parents present, compared with 41 percent of poor Hispanic families and 32 percent of impoverished white families. "In all but 11 states, most black children do not live with both parents. In every state, 7 in 10 white children do."[2]

Divorce helped to drive these numbers in the 1960s and 1970s, but by the 1980s unwed parenthood was largely to blame. Today, more than 70 percent of black children are born to unwed mothers. Only 16 percent of black households are married couples with children, the lowest of any racial group in the United States, while nearly 20 percent are female-headed with children, which is the highest of any group. Like most blacks, my parents knew (if only from the experience of friends and family) all about the strong links between broken homes and bad outcomes. They knew that the likelihood of drug abuse, criminal behavior, teen pregnancy, and dropping out of school increased dramatically when fathers weren't around. And though they couldn't save their marriage, my parents were resolved to save their kids. What this meant in practice was that they tried, with mixed results, to minimize the impact of America's black subculture on their children.

For her part, my mother turned to the church. She was born in Alabama in 1938 and raised Baptist, but became a Jehovah's Witness at the urging of an older sister in the mid-1970s. My mother, my sisters, and I attended services three times a week, and the congregation was integrated but mostly black. That included most of the church elders—married men who held down jobs, provided for their families, didn't smoke or curse, spoke standard English, dressed in suits and ties, and took fatherhood seriously. My mother wanted them to serve as role models for me, and they did, even long after I left the religion voluntarily in my teens. In addition, most of my extended family in Buffalo were members of the church. The aunt who introduced my mother to the religion had adult children who were also Witnesses. Two of her sons were church elders with kids my age; a daughter was married to an elder and they, too, had children being raised in the faith. It was a large, extremely close clan, and the adults were counting on the religion to provide not only spiritual guidance for the children but also something of a refuge from a larger black culture that seemed to be rapidly coarsening.

My father, who was never involved with the religion, thought it most important that his children be educated. He was born in Florida in 1941, but in the 1950s his family move to Newburgh, New York, where he attended high school. He was an outstanding athlete, went to college on a football scholarship, and played profes-sional football in Canada in the 1960s. When his playing days were through he returned to school and obtained a master's degree in social work. I played my share of sports as a kid and he was always there to cheer me on, but Dad was adamant that schoolwork come first.

A year after I was born my parents left a predominantly black neighborhood and purchased a home hard by the University at Buffalo, my father's alma mater. University Heights, as the neigh-borhood was known, was still predominantly white in the 1970s and 1980s—our nonwhite neighbors were mainly foreigners who attended the college or taught there—but black families like ours were starting to move in. Years later I asked my father why he and my mother had quit the black side of town. He told me that they didn't like what blacks were doing to their own communities. He mentioned the crime, the abandoned lots, the graffiti, the litter, the unkempt homes. But his main concern, he said, were the "knuck-leheads" and "thugs" whom he wanted his children far away from. He understood that some families didn't have the means to leave, and he didn't begrudge those who could move, but stayed anyway. But he wasn't taking any chances with his kids.

My father spent most of his professional life working at a local psychiatric hospital run by the state. But he always had other jobs on the side, and they typically kept him in close contact with Buf-falo's black community. He ran a home for troubled boys when he got out of graduate school. Later he ran an after-school tutoring program for low-income kids in a depressed section of town. For a few years he even owned a bar and restaurant in a black neighbor-hood, and was able to provide some economic activity and jobs in the community. But when it came to himself and his family, he didn't want to tempt fate. We lived around whites.

Of course, many of our friends and most of our extended family lived in the black sections of town. Growing up, my best buddy, Trevor, lived on the same street that we had before moving to University Heights. Like my family, Trevor's was middle class. Like me, Trevor had a mother who was a Jehovah's Witness and a father who wasn't. His parents were married; he and his younger sister had a good relationship with their dad; and Trevor was a solid student who excelled in math and science. Buffalo had two selective public high schools that used entrance exams. Trevor attended one of them and his sister attended the other.

But Trevor's neighborhood ultimately got the better of him. Over time, he was taken in by the knuckleheads and thugs. School became less attractive to him than running the streets. He drank and smoked weed. His language and attitude changed. Always a little quiet, he became sullen and much more withdrawn. He listened to gangsta rappers like the Geto Boys and Ice-T. Girls became "bitches." He got into fights. He asked me why I hung out with "white boys." We would cross paths from time to time as teenagers, but by the end of high school I hardly knew Trevor anymore. We lived in different worlds. He kept company with a crowd that I consciously avoided.

At the time, Trevor's "white boys" comment stung. I did have a number of white friends on account of the schools I attended. So long as we could afford it, my father sent me to private institutions, where black students were scarce. I went to public schools in seventh, eighth, eleventh, and twelfth grades, but I wound up in honors classes where the vast majority of kids were white. My two sisters, to my father's chagrin, opted for the neighborhood public schools. Nor did they take to the church, which distressed my mom. Both of them fell in with the wrong crowd, willingly. Indeed, they largely rejected the middle-class values that our parents labored to instill in us. And notwithstanding the geographic distance, soon they were sliding into Trevor's world. We lived under the same roof, but I spoke, dressed, and generally behaved in ways that were not only different from my siblings but associated in their minds with "acting white." The teasing was good-natured for the most part, and I didn't let it get to me, but it was constant throughout my adolescence. It came from friends and family, from children and adults, from fellow congregants in the church, and on one occasion from a black public-high-school teacher who mocked my standard English in front of the entire class after I'd answered a question.

I very much enjoyed school. I was outgoing, athletic, made friends easily. But it wasn't just the social life that attracted me. I also liked learning. I liked books. I was curious about the world. I wanted to be smart, not because I associated it with being white but because I associated it with my father. Dad was smart, and I wanted to be like Dad. I didn't avoid black friendships, but most of the people I came across who shared my sensibilities, particularly about education, were white. There were other studious black kids around, but not many, and there seemed to be fewer as I got older. The reality was that if you were a bookish black kid who placed shared sensibilities above shared skin color, you probably had a lot of white friends.

By contrast, the Trevors were everywhere. I was related to them, attended school with them, worshipped with them. These were black kids from good families who nevertheless fell victim to social pathologies: crime, drugs, teen pregnancies, and a tragically warped sense of what it means to be black. Some were ghetto kids from broken homes with the odds stacked against them. But a surprising number were middle-class children from intact families who chose to reject middle-class values. They were not destined for Buffalo's mean streets. They had options and they knew better. Yet the worst

41

aspects of black culture seemed to find them, win them over, and sometimes destroy their lives. My black peers were getting pregnant and fathering children. My cousins were compiling criminal records and doing drugs. My parents did what they could, but in the end neither the church nor University Heights proved impenetrable. By the time I graduated from high school my older sister was a single mom. By the time I graduated from college my younger sister was dead from a drug overdose. A short time later Trevor would also be dead, and his sister would also be a single mother.

The kind of ribbing that I experienced as a child would follow me into adulthood, where my older sister's children would take to deriding my diction. "Why you talk white, Uncle Jason?" my niece, all of nine years old at the time, once asked me during a visit. Turning to her friend, she continued, "Don't my uncle sound white? Why he trying to sound so smart?" They shared a chuckle at my expense, and I was reminded of how early these self-defeating attitudes take hold. Here were a couple of black third graders already linking speech patterns to race and intelligence. Moreover, they had determined that "sounding white" was something to be mocked in other blacks and avoided in their own speech.

The findings of academics who have researched this "acting white" phenomenon are thoroughly depressing, and demonstrate that my experiences are neither new nor atypical. Here is basketball great Kareem Abdul-Jabbar describing his experience as a studious kid at a predominantly black Catholic school outside of Philadelphia in the 1950s:

I got there and immediately found I could read better than anyone in the school. My father's example and my mother's training had made that come easy; I could pick up a book, read it out loud, pronounce the words with proper inflection and actually know what they meant. When the nuns found this out they paid me a lot of attention, once even asking me, a fourth grader, to read to the seventh grade. When the kids found this out I became a target . . .

It was my first time away from home, my first experience in an all-black situation, and I found myself being punished for doing everything I'd ever been taught was right. I got all A's and was hated for it; I spoke correctly and was called a punk. I had to learn a new language simply to be able to deal with the threats. I had good manners and was a good little boy and paid for it with my hide.[3]

In the late 1990s the black residents of Shaker Heights, Ohio, an affluent Cleveland suburb, invited John Ogbu, professor of anthropology at the University of California, Berkeley, to examine the black-white academic achievement gap in their community. Roughly a third of the town's residents were black, and the school district was divided equally along racial lines. Yet the black kids trailed far behind whites in test scores, grade-point averages, placement in high-level classes, and college attendance. Black students were receiving 80 percent of the Ds and Fs.

Nationwide, the racial gap in education is well documented. Black kids are overrepresented among high-school dropouts and students who are not performing at grade level. Black scores on the SAT and other standardized tests are far lower on average than those of whites. The achievement gap begins in elementary school and widens in higher grades. By the end of high school the typical black student is several years behind his white peers in reading and math. The usual explanation of this is class inequality. Blacks don't perform on the level of whites because they come from a lower socioeconomic background and their schools have fewer resources, goes the argument. But what Ogbu found is that this problem transcends class and persists even among the children of affluent, educated black professionals.

"None of the versions of the class-inequality [argument] can explain why Black students from similar social class backgrounds, residing in the same neighborhood, and attending the same school, don't do as well as White students," wrote Ogbu. "Within the Black population, of course, middle-class children do better, on the average, than lower-class children, just as in the White population. However, when Blacks and Whites from similar socioeconomic backgrounds are compared, one sees that Black students at every class level perform less well in school than their White counterparts."[4]

Ogbu and his team of researchers were given access to parents, teachers, principals, administrators, and students in the Shaker Heights school district, which was one of the country's best. And he concluded that black culture, more than anything else, explained the academic achievement gap. The black kids readily admitted that they didn't work as hard as whites, took easier classes, watched more TV, and read fewer books. "A kind of norm of minimum effort appeared to exist among Black students," wrote Ogbu. "The students themselves recognized this and used it to explain both their academic behaviors and their low academic achievement performance."[5] Due to peer pressure, some black students "didn't work as hard as they should and could." Among their black friends, "it was not cool to be successful" or "to work hard or to show you're smart." One female student said that some black students believed "it was cute to be dumb." Asked why, "she said it was because they couldn't do well and that they didn't want anyone else to do well."[6]

Ogbu found that black high-school students "avoided certain attitudes, standard English, and some behaviors because they considered them White. They feared that adopting White ways would be detrimental to their collective racial identity and solidarity. Unfortunately, some of the attitudes labeled 'White' and avoided by the students were those that enhanced school success." The behaviors and attitudes to be avoided included, for example, enrolling in honors and advanced-placement classes, striving for high grades, talking properly, hanging around too many white students, and participating in extracurricular activities that were populated by whites.

"What amazed me is that these kids who come from homes of doctors and lawyers are not thinking like their parents; they don't know how their parents made it," Ogbu told the *New York Times* in 2002. "They are looking at rappers in ghettos as their role models, they are looking at entertainers. The parents work two jobs, three jobs, to give their children everything, but they are not guiding their children."[7]

Indeed, Ogbu found that it wasn't just the black kids who were academically disengaged. Few black parents were members of the PTO. Participation in early-elementary-school programs designed primarily for black children was spurned by black families. And white parents tended to have higher academic expectations for their kids. "From school personnel reports of school authorities, interviews with students, discussions with parents themselves, and our observations, we can confidently conclude that Black parents in Shaker Heights did not participate actively in school organizations and in school events and programs designed to enhance their children's academic engagement and achievement," he wrote.[8]

But in at least one important respect, Ogbu faulted the school system itself for the achievement gap. It turned out that teachers were passing students who did not perform at grade level. The practice was widespread, particularly in kindergarten through eighth grade, and well known among students. And the teachers who were setting lower standards for black kids had "good intentions," he reported. But it had the effect of leading some black kids to believe that they were doing better in school than they really were. Other kids simply didn't try as hard as they would have otherwise. When Ogbu asked students why their grades were poor, "they would say that they did not take their schoolwork seriously because they knew they were going to be passed into the ninth grade anyway." Ogbu's team of researchers also noted that in classes where most of the kids were black, teachers expected less of the students in terms of homework, even going so far as to de-emphasize its importance. Obviously, school officials aren't responsible for the poor attitudes and lack of effort among black kids, but ignoring or indulging this isn't going to help close the learning gap.

Today's civil rights leaders encourage blacks to see themselves as victims. The overriding message from the NAACP, the National Urban League, and most black politicians is that white racism explains black pathology. Ogbu's research shows that this message is not lost on black youth. "Black students chose well-educated and successful professional Blacks in Shaker Heights and elsewhere in the nation as role models," he noted. "However, the role models were admired because of their leadership in the 'collective struggle' against White oppression or in the civil rights movement rather than because of their academic and professional success or other attributes that made them successful in the corporate economy or wider societal institutions."[9]

There was a time when black leaders understood the primacy of black self-development. They fought hard for equal opportunity, but knew that blacks have to be culturally prepared to take advantage of those opportunities when they arrive. "We know that there are many things wrong in the white world, but there are many things wrong in the black world, too," Martin Luther King Jr. once told a congregation. "We can't keep on blaming the white man. There are things we must do for ourselves." Today we have people trying to help blacks by making excuses for them. Thus, the achievement gap is not the product of a black subculture that rejects attitudes and behaviors conducive to academic success; rather, it results from "racist" standardized tests or "Eurocentric" teaching styles. Multiculturalists like Geneva Gay, a professor of education at the University of Washington–Seattle, tell us that black kids are under-performing in public schools because of how they're being taught.

"Standards of 'goodness' in teaching and learning are culturally determined and are not the same for all ethnic groups," she wrote.

> The structures, assumptions, substance, and operations of conventional educational enterprises are European American cultural icons. A case in point is the protocols of attentiveness and the emphasis placed on them in classrooms. Students are expected to pay close attention to teachers for a prolonged, largely uninterrupted length of time. Specific signs and signals have evolved that are associated with appropriate attentive behaviors. These include nonverbal communicative cues, such as gaze, eye contact, and body posture. When they are not exhibited . . . students are [unfairly] judged to be uninvolved, distracted, having short attention spans, and/or engaged in off-task behaviors.

Gay said that if the U.S. school system would do a better job of accommodating the "cultural orientations, values and performance styles of ethnically different students" instead of "imposing cultural hegemony," then black kids would "feel less compelled to sabotage or camouflage their academic achievement to avoid compromising their cultural and ethnic integrity."[10] In other words, black kids are being asked to sit still in class, pay attention, follow rules, and complete homework assignments—all of which is a huge imposition on them, if not a racist expectation.

One major problem with this theory is that it can't explain the performance of other nonwhite students, including black immigrants, who readily adjust to the pedagogic methods of U.S. schools and go on to outperform black Americans. Even black immigrants for whom English is a second language have managed to excel in U.S. schools. When public-school officials in Seattle (which is home to a significant number of African foreign nationals) broke down test scores by specific home language, they found that "African-American students whose primary language is English perform significantly worse in math and reading than black students who speak another language at home—typically immigrants or refugees." Just 36 percent of black students who speak English at home passed their grade's math exam, compared to 47 percent of Somali-speaking students. In reading, 56 percent of black students who speak English passed, while 67 percent of Somali-speaking students passed. And kids from Ethiopia and Eritrea scored even higher than the Somali students.[11] A 2007 study published in the *American Journal of Education* found that although immigrants were just 13 percent of the U.S. population, they accounted for more than a quarter of the black students at the nation's twenty-eight most selective colleges and universities. If "Eurocentric" teaching methods, rather than cultural values, explain poor academic outcomes among black natives, how to explain the relative success of black immigrants from backgrounds much more foreign than those of their U.S. counterparts?

Another nonwhite group that has thrived academically despite supposedly biased teaching methods is Asians. More than half of the 14,400 students enrolled in New York City's eight specialized high schools in 2012 were Asian, even though Asians make up just 14 percent of the city's public-school students. To appreciate their dominance, consider the racial makeup of the city's three most selective public schools—Stuyvesant High School, the Bronx High School of Science, and Brooklyn Technical High School—all of which require an admissions test. In 2013 Stuyvesant, which is 70 percent Asian, offered admission to 9 black students, 177 white students, and 620 students who identified as Asian. The breakdown at Bronx Science was 25 blacks, 239 whites, and 489 Asians. At Brooklyn Tech, the numbers were 110, 451, and 960, respectively.[12]

What's remarkable about the racial differences is that while most of the black and white kids at these schools come from middle-class and affluent families, many of the Asians are immigrants, or the children of immigrants from low-income households where English isn't the first language spoken or in some cases isn't even spoken at all. When WNYC, the local NPR affiliate in New York, looked at 2012 admissions data for these selective schools, it found that a disproportionate number of the students lived in an Asian immigrant community in Brooklyn. "An analysis by WNYC found more than 300 students from three zip codes in the vicinity got into the city's specialized high schools last year," the radio station reported.

> Those three zip codes include parts of Sunset Park, Borough Park and Dyker Heights. They were among the 20 zip codes with the most acceptances to the elite high schools. Yet, the average incomes in those three zip codes are low enough for a

family of four to qualify for free lunch (they range from about $35,000-$40,000 a year). That's striking because most of the other admissions to the elite schools came from middle to upper class neighborhoods.

The report went on to explain how diligently the families prepare for these admissions tests. It turns out that the most popular weekend activity for middle-school students is test preparation. While the parents work six or seven days a week in menial, labor-intensive jobs, the children, beginning in sixth grade or earlier, are preparing for high-school entrance exams. "Even the lowest paid immigrants scrape up enough money for tutoring because those high schools are seen as the ticket to a better life."[13] The parents push the children to do well academically, and the students in turn encourage one another. The culture places a high value on education, and the results speak for themselves. So while multiculturalists are busy complaining about teaching methods and civil rights leaders are busy complaining about standardized tests, the Asian kids are busy studying.

Education is not the only area where an oppositional black mindset has been detrimental to social and economic progress. Black cultural attitudes toward work, authority, dress, sex, and violence have also proven counterproductive, inhibiting the development of the kind of human capital that has lead to socioeconomic advancement for other groups. But it's hard to see how blacks will improve their lot without changing their attitudes toward school. A culture that takes pride in ignorance and mocks learnedness has a dim future. And those who attempt to make excuses for black social pathology rather than condemning these behaviors in no uncertain terms are part of the problem. "The middle-class values by which we [middle-class blacks] were raised—the work ethic, the importance of education, the value of property ownership, of respectability, of 'getting ahead,' of stable family life, of initiative, of self-reliance, et cetera—are, in themselves, raceless and even assimilationist," wrote race scholar Shelby Steele. "But the particular pattern of racial identification that emerged in the sixties and that still prevails today urges middle-class blacks (and all blacks) in the opposite direction. This pattern asks us to see ourselves as an embattled minority."[14]

Black culture today not only condones delinquency and thuggery but celebrates it to the point where black youths have adopted jail fashion in the form of baggy, low-slung pants and oversize T-shirts. Hip-hop music immortalizes drug dealers and murderers. On a 2013 album Jay-Z, one of the country's richest and most popular rappers, referenced one Wayne Perry in a song. Perry was a hit man in the 1980s for one of Washington, D.C.'s most notorious drug lords. He pleaded guilty in 1994 to five murders, and received five consecutive life sentences. In an interview with *Rolling Stone* magazine in 2010, President Barack Obama expressed his affinity for rappers like Jay-Z and Lil Wayne, whose lyrics often elevate misogyny, drug dealing, and gun violence. At the time of the president's interview, Lil Wayne was imprisoned on gun and drug charges.

Rappers have long expressed pride in spreading degeneracy among black youths. "You walk into a fourth or fifth grade black school today," Chuck D of Public Enemy told the *Village Voice* in 1991, "I'm telling you, you're finding chaos right now, 'cause rappers came in the game and threw that confusing element in it, and kids is like, Yo, fuck this."[15] Meanwhile, liberal sages are preoccupied with "contextualizing" this cultural rot. Cornel West describes rap as "primarily the musical expression of the paradoxical cry of desperation and celebration of the black underclass and poor working class, a cry that openly acknowledges and confronts the wave of personal coldheartedness, criminal cruelty and existential hopeless-ness in the black ghettos."[16] Michael Eric Dyson, the sociologist and television commentator who credits rappers with "refining the art of oral communication," says that "before we discard the genre, we should understand that gangsta rap often reaches higher than its ugliest, lowest common denominator. Misogyny, violence, materi-alism, and sexual transgression are not its exclusive domain. At its best, this music draws attention to complex dimensions of ghetto life ignored by many Americans."[17] Psychiatrists James Comer and Alvin Poussaint tell parents that the nonstop profanity used by black kids today is nothing to get worked up over. "Profanity is profanity, period, and not part of the black language style. On the other hand, you should not let words like fuck, shit, ass, and motherfucker cause you to have seizures, see red, or run for the Bible," the authors explain. "Today the use of 'motherfucker' has so changed that some young blacks use it as a term of endearment and respect. The terms 'shit,' 'bitch,' and 'nigger' also serve as both epithets and expressions of endearment within sections of the black community."[18]

Black intellectuals, it seems, are much more interested in attacking those who are critical of these black cultural expressions. When black officials in Louisiana and Georgia moved to pass inde-cency laws aimed at the proliferation of youths who refused to cover their backsides in public, Dyson criticized not the kids or the culture but the proposals, telling the *New York Times* that proponents had "bought the myth that sagging pants represents an offensive lifestyle which leads to destructive behavior." And Benjamin Chavis, the former head of the NAACP, vowed to challenge the ordinances in court. "I think to criminalize how a person wears their clothing is more offensive than what the remedy is trying to do," said Chavis.[19]

In 2004 the comedian Bill Cosby was the featured speaker at an NAACP awards ceremony commemorating the fiftieth anniversary of the Supreme Court's landmark *Brown v. Board of Education* decision. Cosby used the occasion to offer a stinging critique of contemporary black culture. He said that blacks today are squandering the gains of the civil rights movement, and white racism is not to blame. "We, as black folks, have to do a better job," he stated. "We have to start holding each other to a higher standard." Today in our cities, he said,

> *we have 50 percent [school] dropout [rates] in our neighborhoods. We have . . . men in prison. No longer is a person embarrassed because [she is] pregnant without a husband. No longer is a boy considered an embarrassment if he tries to run away from being the father.*

Here are some other excerpts from Cosby's address:

> *People putting their clothes on backwards—isn't that a sign of something going on wrong? Aren't you paying attention? People with their hats on backwards, pants down around the crack . . .*
>
> *Everybody knows it's important to speak English except these knuckleheads. You can't land a plane with "Why you ain't . . . " You can't be a doctor with that kind of crap coming out of your mouth. There is no Bible that has that kind of language. Where did these people get the idea that they're moving ahead on this . . . these people are fighting hard to be ignorant.*
>
> *Five or six different children—same woman, eight, ten different husbands or whatever. Pretty soon you're going to have to have DNA cards so you can tell who you're making love to . . .*

What the hell good is Brown v. Board of Education *if nobody wants it?*[20]

Cosby received a standing ovation from the audience that evening, but the black intelligentsia wasn't so kind. Dyson took him to task for "elitist viewpoints" that overemphasized personal responsibility and "reinforce[d] suspicions about black humanity."[21] The playwright August Wilson said he was "a billionaire attacking poor people for being poor. Bill Cosby is a clown. What do you expect?" Theodore Shaw, then head of the NAACP Legal Defense Fund, said the speech was a "harsh attack on poor black people" that ignored "systemic" racism. Commentator Ta-Nehisi Coates agreed, noting that the legacy of slavery and Jim Crow—that is, the actions of whites—was primarily responsible for black behavior today, and that "Cosby's argument—that much of what haunts young black men originates in post-segregation black culture—doesn't square with history."[22]

Actually, it does. In Philadelphia circa 1880, 75 percent of black families and 73 percent of white families were comprised of two parents and children. In Philadelphia circa 2007, "married-couple families account for only 34 percent of African American family households, while white married-couple families account for 68 percent of white family households," according to the Urban League of Philadelphia. Was there less racism in America, structural or otherwise, fifteen years after the end of the Civil War than there was a year before Barack Obama was elected president? In 1847 Philadelphia—that is, prior to the end of slavery—historians report, two-parent families were more common among ex-slaves than freeborn blacks. And Philadelphia was no outlier. Nationwide, data from every census taken between 1890 and 1940 show the black marriage rate exceeding the white rate. Liberals want to blame the "legacy" of slavery and racism for the breakdown of the black family and subsequent social pathologies. But the empirical data support Bill Cosby.

There is a much stronger case to be made that efforts to *help* blacks have had more pernicious and lasting effects on black attitudes and habits than either slavery or segregation. Social welfare programs that were initiated or greatly expanded during the 1960s resulted in the government effectively displacing black fathers as breadwinners, and made work less attractive. Even before Lyndon Johnson's War on Poverty began in earnest, New York and other states had already been expanding their social welfare programs. And despite the best intentions, the results were not encouraging.

"The number of abandoned families had grown enormously in the 1960s," explained Harvard social scientist Nathan Glazer.

> *More liberal welfare eligibility and benefits were one factor that had encouraged this increase. More generally, the constraints that traditionally kept families together had weakened. In some groups they may not have been strong to begin with. Our efforts to soften the harsh consequences of family breakup spoke well of our compassion and concern, but these efforts also made it easier for fathers to abandon their families or mothers to disengage from their husbands.*[23]

Moreover, these efforts were taking place during a period of civil rights gains and declining anti-black bias, as Daniel Patrick Moynihan explained to an interviewer in 1967:

> *In the South . . . there were a great many outcomes—situations, customs, rules—which were inimical to Negro rights, which*

violated Negro rights and which were willed *outcomes. Intended, planned, desired outcomes. And it was, therefore, possible to seek out those individuals who were willing the outcomes and to coerce them to cease to do so.*

Now, you come to New York City, with its incomparable expenditures on education; and you find that, in the twelfth grade, Negro students are performing at the sixth grade level in mathematics. Find me the man who wills that outcome. Find the legislator who has held back money, the teacher who's held back his skills, the school superintendent who's deliberately discriminating, the curriculum supervisor who puts the wrong books in, the architect who builds the bad schools. He isn't there![24]

Ideally, welfare dependency should be a passing phase, and for most people it is. But for too many black families it has become the norm, and even those who escape it often return. The *Economist* magazine, citing a 2011 Chicago Federal Reserve study, noted that "roughly 60% of black Americans whose parents had an above-average income fell below the average as adults. The figure for whites was 36%."[25] An earlier Pew study found that some 45 percent of blacks (versus 15 percent of whites) who were born into the middle class in the 1960s had slid into poverty or near-poverty. Since it is unlikely that the effects of slavery and Jim Crow are hopscotching generations, perhaps something else is to blame. By retarding or otherwise interfering with black self-development, government programs have tended to do more harm than good. And black elites who choose to focus on the behavior of whites are encouraging these youngsters to do the same, and thus perpetuating the problem.

A sad irony of the black cultural obsession with avoiding white behavior is that the habits and attitudes associated with ghetto life today can be traced not to Mother Africa but to Europeans who immigrated to the American South. From 1790 until the Civil War, approximately half of the white population of the South "was of Irish, Scottish, or Welsh extraction, and about half of the remainder had originated in the western and northern English uplands," according to Grady McWhiney's *Cracker Culture*. These immigrants brought their Old World habits and patterns to America and passed them along to the people who lived around them, which included most black people in America. Social critics of the period, including Frederick Law Olmstead and Alexis de Tocqueville, contrasted the behavior of these immigrants with those from other regions of Europe who settled in the northern United States. So have modern-day scholars of nineteenth-century Southern culture, like McWhiney, Forrest McDonald, and David Hackett Fischer. And what's fascinating about their descriptions is how much they resemble black ghetto culture today. In the opening essay of his 2005 book, *Black Rednecks and White Liberals*, Thomas Sowell neatly summarized some of these findings:

> *The cultural values and social patterns prevalent among Southern whites included an aversion to work, proneness to violence, neglect of education, sexual promiscuity, improvidence, drunkenness, lack of entrepreneurship, reckless searches for excitement, lively music and dance, and a style of religious oratory marked by strident rhetoric, unbridled emotions, and flamboyant imagery. This oratorical style carried over into the political oratory of the region in both the Jim Crow era and the civil rights era, and has continued on into our own times among black politicians, preachers, and activists.*[26]

Most whites have of course abandoned this behavior, and have risen socioeconomically as a result. How ironic that so many blacks cling to these practices in an effort to avoid "acting white." And how tragic that so many liberals choose to put an intellectual gloss on black cultural traits that deserve disdain. The civil rights movement, properly understood, was about equal opportunity. But a group must be culturally equipped to seize it. Blacks today on balance remain ill equipped, and the problem isn't white people.

03

THE ENEMY
WITHIN

During the summer of 1993, between my junior and senior years of college, I worked as an intern at *USA Today*. The newspaper's offices were located in northern Virginia, just outside of Washington, D.C., but I stayed with an aunt and uncle who lived on the other side of the District, in Maryland. I owned a car and drove to the office, and since I was assigned to the sports desk I often didn't leave work until well after midnight, once the West Coast baseball games had been completed.

The fastest way home was straight though D.C., though my uncle had warned me that it wasn't the safest route at that time of night. In the early 1990s Washington was dubbed the "murder capital" because it led the country in per capita homicides. But then, 21-year-old males aren't exactly known for being risk averse or heeding advice from their elders. Sure enough, one night after work, around 1 a.m., I was sitting at a red light when no fewer than four squad cars converged on me, lights flashing and sirens screaming. Seconds later police officers were pointing guns at me as I sat cowering in my Volkswagen Fox. I was ordered to exit the vehicle, to face away from it, and to place my hands on my head. I was not-so-gently pushed to the pavement facedown, then handcuffed and searched, along with the car, while two officers kept their weapons trained on me. When the police finished I was told that I had fit the description of someone they were after, something about me having New York license plates and problems with gunrunners from up North. They apologized and were gone as fast as they had arrived.

I remember getting back into my car and just sitting there in a daze, sweating. The engine was off and the windows were up and it was a muggy summer night. Eventually another car pulled up to the light behind me and honked because I wasn't moving. I pulled over to the curb, collected myself and the items from my glove compartment (mostly cassette tapes) that D.C.'s finest had left in the passenger seat and on the floor, and then I drove home. I changed my route home the next day and never doubted my uncle again.

It was certainly the most terrifying encounter I'd had with the police, but it wasn't the first or the last. Growing up in Buffalo, New York, in the 1980s I was stopped several times by the cops while walking alone through white residential neighborhoods where friends lived. When the police asked what I was doing there and I told them, sometimes they wanted the family's name for verification. As a youngster I wondered if these neighborhoods were so well policed that cops really did know the names of everyone who lived there, or whether they just wanted me to think that they did. I don't know if the police stopped me of their own volition, or whether a neighbor looking out his window had spotted an unfamiliar black kid and dialed 911. I never asked.

The summer I graduated from high school my father helped me buy a car—the aforementioned VW—and the first thing I did was head over to the home of a former classmate to show him my new ride. I noticed a police car following me as I turned off the thoroughfare and headed into my friend's neighborhood. I had to make several more turns to reach his block, and the cop turned every time I did. Naturally, I started getting nervous. Finally, about four houses from my destination, he hit the siren. The officer walked up to my car and asked me where I was headed. I pointed to the house. Then he looked at the temporary registration on my windshield and asked, "What's that?" I said the car was new and that I was still waiting for the permanent registration to come in the mail. The officer told me to wait while he checked out my story. So I waited.

It was a warm and sunny Saturday afternoon. People—white people—were outside. Neighbors were chatting. Kids were playing in their front yards. And now everyone had paused to stare at me, this young black guy who'd just been pulled over by the police. When homeowners look outside and see cops, they get curious. When they see cops stopping a black kid, they get nervous. The officer finally came back to the car and told me I was free to go, but I no longer had any interest in showing my friend my new car. I just wanted to get out of that neighborhood, which is probably what that cop wanted, and thanks to him, probably what everyone else on that street who witnessed our encounter wanted. I obliged.

These episodes would continue in college. While attending the University at Buffalo, where I lived off campus, I was stopped regularly while driving through the main drag of a tony suburb on my way to morning classes. I would hand over my license and registration and then sit in the car for ten minutes or so while the officers did whatever they do while you wait. I was never ticketed during these stops, or even told that I did anything wrong. I didn't ask why I was being pulled over and the officers didn't feel the need to volunteer an explanation. Sometimes I wouldn't be pulled over, just tailed by a police cruiser until I reached the town line. But I was stopped often enough that I eventually started taking a different route to campus, even though it added ten to fifteen minutes to the trip.

Like so many other young black men, I was also followed in department stores, saw people cross the street as I approached, and watched women clutch their purses in elevators when they didn't simply decide to ride a different one. It was part of growing up. As a teenager I didn't dress like a thug or go around scowling at people. I tucked in my shirts, embraced belts, and had no pressing desire to show others my underpants. My closet was full of khakis, button-downs, and crew-neck sweaters (still is), and when I donned a baseball cap it was turned the right way. My VW looked like a VW. It wasn't tricked out with chrome rims and tinted windows. When I played music in my car, it ran to De La Soul and Talking Heads rather than Ice Cube, and in any case could not be heard several blocks away. All of which is to say that my suspicion-raising features, when it came to cops or pedestrians, obviously were my race and my age (and I gather mostly the latter, since the harassment stopped decades ago and I'm still as black as I was at 17). Was I profiled based on negative stereotypes about young black men? Almost certainly. But then everyone profiles based on limited knowledge, including me.

In high school I worked as a stock boy in a supermarket. The people caught stealing were almost always black. As a result black shoppers got more scrutiny from everyone, including black workers. During college I worked the overnight shift at a gas station with a minimart. Again, the people I caught stealing were almost always black. So when people who looked like me entered the store my antenna went up. Similarly, when I see groups of young black men walking down the street at night I cross to the other side. When I see them on subways I switch cars. I am not judging them as individuals. Why take the risk? If I guess wrong my wife is a widow and my children are fatherless. So I make snap judgments with incomplete information.

My attitude and behavior are hardly unique, even among other blacks. Like white cabdrivers, black cabdrivers have been known to avoid picking up black males at night, something I also experienced firsthand upon moving to New York City after college. Black restaurant owners ask groups of young black diners to prepay for their meals, seat them away from the exit, or take other steps to make sure that the bill is settled. And the lady who is nervous about sharing an elevator with a black man might be black herself. Describing her numerous conversations about racial perceptions with other black women, former Spelman College president Johnnetta Cole wrote, "One of the most painful admissions I hear is: I am afraid of my own people."[1]

Some individuals who avoid encounters with black youths may indeed be acting out of racism, but given that law-abiding blacks exhibit the exact same behavior it's likely that most people are acting on probability. "If I'm walking down a street in Center City Philadelphia at two in the morning and I hear some footsteps behind me and I turn around and there are a couple of young white dudes behind me, I am probably not going to get very uptight. I am probably not going to have the same reaction if I turn around and there is the proverbial black urban youth behind me," Theodore McKee, a black federal judge, told an interviewer in the 1990s. "Now, if I can have this reaction—and I'm a black male who has studied martial arts for twenty some odd years and can defend myself—I can't help but think that the average white judge in the situation will have a reaction that is ten times more intense."[2] (When the interviewer, Linn Washington, also black, was asked on C-SPAN to respond to the judge's remarks, he said, "I can relate to it because I ride the subways in Philadelphia late at night.")[3]

My encounters with law enforcement growing up were certainly frustrating; I was getting hassled for the past behavior of other blacks. But that doesn't necessarily make those encounters arbitrary or unreasonable. After all, perceptions of black criminality are based on the reality of high black crime rates. I say that as though it's a given, and it is a given in the real world. But in the alternate universe of academia and the liberal mainstream media, there is still a raging debate over whether people's fears of young black men have anything at all to do with the actual behavior of young black men.

Michelle Alexander, an associate professor of law at Ohio State University, has written an entire book, *The New Jim Crow*, that blames high black incarceration rates on racial discrimination. She posits that prisons are teeming with young black men due primarily to a war on drugs that was launched by the Reagan administration in the 1980s for the express purpose of resegregating society. "This book argues that mass incarceration is, metaphorically, the New Jim

Crow and that all those who care about social justice should fully commit themselves to dismantling this new racial caste system," wrote Alexander.[4] "What this book is intended to do—the only thing it is intended to do—is to stimulate a much-needed conversation about the role of the criminal justice system in creating and perpetrating racial hierarchy in the United States."[5] Liberals love to have "conversations" about these matters, and Alexander got her wish. The book was a best seller. NPR interviewed her multiple times at length. The *New York Times* said that Alexander "deserved to be compared to Du Bois." The *San Francisco Chronicle* described the book as "The Bible of a social movement."

But the conversation that Alexander wants to have glosses over the fact that black men commit a hugely disproportionate number of crimes in the United States. *The New Jim Crow* is chock-full of data on the racial makeup of prisons, but you will search in vain for anything approaching a sustained discussion of black crime rates. To Alexander and those who share her view, the two are largely unrelated. Black incarceration rates, she wrote, result from "a stunningly comprehensive and well-disguised system of racialized social control."[6] The author seems reluctant even to acknowledge that black people behind bars have done anything wrong. In her formulation, blacks are simply "far more likely to be labeled criminals"[7] and are as blameless as slaves in the antebellum South. "When we say someone was 'treated like a criminal,' what we mean to say is that he or she was treated as less than human, like a shameful creature," Alexander wrote. "Hundreds of years ago, our nation put those considered less than human in shackles; less than one hundred years ago, we relegated them to the other side of town; today we put them in cages."[8] Really?

When *I* say that someone is being treated like a criminal, I mean that person is being treated like he broke the law or otherwise did something wrong. (When I want to say someone is being treated as less than human, I say that person is being treated like an animal, not a criminal.) Her chattel slavery and Jim Crow analogies are similarly tortured and yet another effort to explain away stark racial differences in criminality. But unlike prisons, those institutions punished people for being black, not for misbehaving. (A slave who never broke the law remained a slave.) Yet Alexander insists that we blame police and prosecutors and drug laws and societal failures—anything except individual behavior—and even urges the reader to reject the notion of black free will. "The temptation is to insist that black men 'choose' to be criminals," she wrote. "The myth of choice here is seductive, but it should be resisted."[9] What Alexander and others who buy her arguments are really asking us to resist are not myths but realities—namely, which groups are more likely to commit crimes and how such trends drive the negative racial stereotypes that are so prevalent among blacks and nonblacks alike.

In the summer of 2013, after neighborhood watchman George Zimmerman, a Hispanic, was acquitted in the shooting death of Trayvon Martin, an unarmed black teenager, the political left wanted to have a discussion about everything except the black crime rates that lead people to view young black males with suspicion. President Obama and Attorney General Holder wanted to talk about gun control. The NAACP wanted to talk about racial profiling. Assorted academics and MSNBC talking heads wanted to discuss poverty, "stand-your-ground" laws, unemployment, and the supposedly racist criminal justice system. But any candid debate on race and criminality in the United States must begin with the fact that blacks are responsible for an astoundingly disproportionate number of crimes, which has been the case for at least the past half a century.

Crime began rising precipitously in the 1960s after the Supreme Court, under Chief Justice Earl Warren, started tilting the scales in favor of the criminals. Some 63 percent of respondents to a Gallup poll taken in 1968 judged the Warren Court, in place from 1953 to 1969, too lenient on crime; but Warren's jurisprudence was supported wholeheartedly by the Michelle Alexanders of that era, as well as by liberal politicians who wanted to shift blame for criminal behavior away from the criminals. Progressives said that eliminating poverty and racism is the key to lowering crime rates. "You're not going to make this a better America just because you build more jails. What this country needs are more decent neighborhoods, more educated people, better homes," said Hubert Humphrey while campaigning for president in 1968. "I do not believe repression alone can build a better society."[10] Popular books of the time, like Karl Menninger's *The Crime of Punishment*, argued that "law and order" was an "inflammatory" term with racial overtones. "What it really means," said Menninger, "is that we should all go out and find the niggers and beat them up."[11]

"The lenient turn of the mid-twentieth century was, in part, the product of judges, prosecutors, and politicians who saw criminal punishment as too harsh a remedy for ghetto violence," wrote the late William Stuntz, a law professor at Harvard.

The Supreme Court's expansion of criminal defendants' legal rights in the 1960s and after flowed from the Justices' perception that poor and black defendants were being victimized by a system run by white government officials. Even the rise of harsh drug laws was in large measure the product of reformers' efforts to limit the awful costs illegal drug markets impose on poor city neighborhoods. Each of these changes flowed, in large measure, from the decisions of men who saw themselves as reformers. But

*their reforms showed an uncanny ability to take bad situations
and make them worse.*[12]

Crime rates rose by 139 percent during the 1960s, and the
murder rate doubled. Cities couldn't hire cops fast enough. "The
number of police per 1,000 people was up twice the rate of the
population growth, and yet clearance rates for crimes dropped 31
percent and conviction rates were down 6 percent," wrote Lucas A.
Powe Jr. in his history of the Warren Court. "During the last weeks
of his [1968] presidential campaign, Nixon had a favorite line in his
standard speech. 'In the past 45 minutes this is what happened in
America. There has been one murder, two rapes, forty-five major
crimes of violence, countless robberies and auto thefts.'"[13]

As remains the case today, blacks in the past were overrepresented among those arrested and imprisoned. In urban areas in
1967 blacks were seventeen times more likely than whites to be
arrested for robbery. In 1980 blacks comprised about one-eighth
of the population but were half of all those arrested for murder,
rape, and robbery, according to FBI data. And they were between
one-fourth and one-third of all those arrested for crimes such as
burglary, auto theft, and aggravated assault. Today blacks are about
13 percent of the population and continue to be responsible for an
inordinate amount of crime. Between 1976 and 2005 blacks committed more than half of all murders in the United States. The
black arrest rate for most offenses—including robbery, aggravated
assault, and property crimes—is still typically two to three times
their representation in the population. Blacks as a group are also
overrepresented among persons arrested for so-called white-collar
crimes such as counterfeiting, fraud, and embezzlement. And
blaming this decades-long, well-documented trend on racist cops,

prosecutors, judges, sentencing guidelines, and drug laws doesn't cut it as a plausible explanation.

"Even allowing for the existence of discrimination in the criminal justice system, the higher rates of crime among black Americans cannot be denied," wrote James Q. Wilson and Richard Herrnstein in their classic 1985 study, *Crime and Human Nature*. "Every study of crime using official data shows blacks to be overrepresented among persons arrested, convicted, and imprisoned for street crimes." This was true decades before the authors put it to paper, and it remains the case decades later. "The overrepresentation of blacks among arrested persons persists throughout the criminal justice system," wrote Wilson and Herrnstein. "Though prosecutors and judges may well make discriminatory judgments, such decisions do not account for more than a small fraction of the overrepresentation of blacks in prison."[14] Yet liberal policy makers and their allies in the press and the academy consistently downplay the empirical data on black criminal behavior, when they bother to discuss it at all. Stories about the racial makeup of prisons are commonplace; stories about the excessive amount of black criminality are much harder to come by.

"High rates of black violence in the late twentieth century are a matter of historical fact, not bigoted imagination," wrote William Stuntz. "The trends reached their peak not in the land of Jim Crow but in the more civilized North, and not in the age of segregation but in the decades that saw the rise of civil rights for African Americans—and of African American control of city governments."[15] The left wants to blame these outcomes on racial animus and "the system," but blacks have long been part of running that system. Black crime and incarceration rates spiked in the 1970s and '80s in cities such as Baltimore, Cleveland, Detroit, Chicago, Philadelphia,

Los Angeles, and Washington under black mayors and black police chiefs. Some of the most violent cities in the United States today are run by blacks.

The Manhattan Institute's Heather Mac Donald is one of the few journalists who has been willing to write about race and crime honestly, despite the unpopularity of doing so. In books, op-eds, and magazine articles she has picked apart the media's disingenuous coverage of the issue. The *New York Times*, for example, regularly runs stories about racial disparities in police stops while glossing over the racial disparities in crime rates. "Disclosing crime rates— the proper benchmark against which police behavior must be measured—would demolish a cornerstone of the *Times*'s worldview: that the New York Police Department, like police departments across America, oppresses the city's black population with unjustified racial tactics," wrote Mac Donald. In one instance, the *Times* made a very big deal of the fact that in 2009 blacks were 23 percent of the city's population but 55 percent of those stopped by the police. By contrast, whites were 35 percent of the population but accounted for only 10 percent of stops. What the story left out, noted Mac Donald, is that

> blacks committed 66 percent of all violent crimes in the first half of 2009 (though they were only 55 percent of all stops and only 23 percent of the city's population). Blacks committed 80 percent of all shootings in the first half of 2009. Together, blacks and Hispanics committed 98 percent of all shootings. Blacks committed nearly 70 percent of all robberies. Whites, by contrast, committed 5 percent of all violent crimes in the first half of 2009, thought they are 35 percent of the city's population (and were 10 percent of all stops). They committed 1.8 percent of all shootings

and less than 5 percent of all robberies. The face of violent crime in New York, in other words, like in every other large American city, is almost exclusively black and brown.[16]

Critics insist that blacks are overrepresented among those arrested because police focus on black communities, but data consistently show little if any difference between the rate at which victims report the racial identities of their attackers and the rate at which police arrest people of different races. As Mac Donald noted, "No one has come up with a plausible argument as to why crime victims would be biased in their reports."[17] Nor is there any evidence to support the claim that prosecutors are overcharging blacks—or that judges are oversentencing blacks—for the same crimes committed by nonblacks. Mac Donald wrote:

Backing up this bias claim has been the holy grail of criminology for decades—and the prize remains as elusive as ever. In 1997, criminologists Robert Sampson and Janet Lauritsen reviewed the massive literature on charging and sentencing. They concluded that "large racial differences in criminal offending," not racism, explained why more blacks were in prison proportionately than whites and for longer terms. A 1987 analysis of Georgia felony convictions, for example, found that blacks frequently received disproportionately lenient punishment. A 1990 study of 11,000 California cases found that slight racial disparities in sentence length resulted from blacks' prior records and other legally relevant variables. A 1994 Justice Department survey of felony cases from the country's 75 largest urban areas discovered that blacks actually had a lower chance of prosecution following a felony than whites did and that they were less likely to be found guilty at trial. Following conviction, blacks were more likely to receive prison sentences, however—an outcome that reflected the gravity of their offenses as well as their criminal records.[18]

What about the contention that racist drug laws are driving black incarceration rates? Might that help explain why blacks are 13 percent of the population but half of all prison inmates? In 1986, in response to the crack cocaine epidemic that was crushing American inner cities, Congress passed the Anti-Drug Abuse Act, which instituted harsher penalties for crack cocaine offenses than for powder cocaine offenses. For sentencing purposes, the law stipulated that one gram of crack cocaine be treated as equivalent to 100 grams of powder cocaine. Because crack cocaine offenders tended to be black and powder cocaine offenders tended to be white, critics of the law denounced it as racially biased in hindsight. But it's worth remembering that black lawmakers led the initial effort to pass the legislation. The harsher penalties for crack cocaine offenses were supported by most of the Congressional Black Caucus, including New York Representatives Major Owens of Brooklyn and Charles Rangel of Harlem, who at the time headed the House Select Committee on Narcotics Abuse and Control. Crack was destroying black communities, and many black political leaders wanted dealers to face longer sentences. "Eleven of the twenty-one blacks who were then members of the House of Representatives voted in favor of the law which created the 100-to-1 crack–powder differential," noted Harvard law professor Randall Kennedy. "In light of charges that the crack–powder distinction was enacted partly because of conscious or unconscious racism, it is noteworthy that *none* of the black members of Congress made that claim at the time the bill was initially discussed." Kennedy added: "The absence of any charge by black members of Congress that the crack–powder differential was racially unfair speaks volumes; after all, several of these representatives had long histories of distinguished opposition to any public policy that smacked of racial injustice. That several of these representatives demanded a crackdown on crack is also significant. It suggests that the initiative for what became the crack–powder distinction originated to some extent *within* the ranks of African-American congressional officials."[19]

Despite this history, the crack–powder sentencing disparity would, over the next quarter century, become one of the left's favorite examples of America's racist criminal justice system. Barack Obama criticized the law while running for president in 2008 and early in his first term moved to lessen the differential. That effort culminated in the Fair Sentencing Act of 2010, which lowered the ratio to 18 to 1. This was no doubt great news for criminals, but what's been lost in the discussion is whether such a change leaves law-abiding blacks better off. In 2009 blacks were 85 percent of crack offenders, and sentences for crack offenses averaged twenty-four months longer than those for powder cocaine. Civil rights groups and others who equate racial disparities with racism have used such data to decry the sentencing guidelines as racially unjust, yet they don't seem overly concerned with whether blacks in the main are helped or hurt when crack dealers are locked up longer for pushing a substance that has devastated urban black neighborhoods. Why is their sympathy with the lawbreakers?

Celebrated left-wing academics like Michelle Alexander reluctantly acknowledge that "some black mayors, politicians, and lobbyists—as well as preachers, teachers, barbers, and ordinary folk—endorse 'get tough' tactics" by police and the courts that facilitate the high black incarceration rates that she laments. But is it any great shock that black people without advanced degrees have less sympathy for black thugs? The black homicide rate is seven times that of whites, and the George Zimmermans of the world are not the reason. Some 90 percent of black murder victims are killed by other blacks. Why should we care more about black criminals than their black victims? Still, Alexander dismisses tough-on-crime blacks as ignorant and "confused." Of course, the very fact that so many blacks support locking up black criminals undermines her Jim Crow and slavery analogies, since those institutions never had anywhere near the same level of black support. But Alexander is not about to let such petty details stand in her way. "The fact that many African Americans . . . insist that the problems of the urban poor can be best explained by their behavior, culture, and attitude does not, in any meaningful way, distinguish mass incarceration from its [slavery and Jim Crow] predecessors," she wrote.[20]

Liberal elites would have us deny what black ghetto residents know to be the truth. These communities aren't dangerous because of racist cops or judges or sentencing guidelines. They're dangerous mainly due to black criminals preying on black victims. Nor is the racial disparity in prison inmates explained by the enforcement of drug laws. In 2006 blacks were 37.5 percent of the 1,274,600 people in state prisons, which house 88 percent of the nation's prison population, explained Heather Mac Donald. "If you remove drug prisoners from that population, the percentage of black prisoners drops to 37 percent—half of a percentage point, hardly a significant difference." It's true that drug prosecutions have risen markedly over the past thirty years. Drug offenders were 6.4 percent of state prison inmates in 1979 but had jumped to 20 percent by 2004. "Even so," wrote Mac Donald, "violent and property offenders continue to dominate the ranks: in 2004, 52 percent of state prisoners were serving time for violence and 21 percent for property crimes, for a combined total over three and a half times that of state drug offenders." Drug-war critics like to focus on federal prisons, where

74

drug offenders climbed from 25 percent of the inmate population in 1980 to 47.6 percent in 2006. "But the federal system held just 12.3 percent of the nation's prisoners in 2006," noted Mac Donald. "So much for the claim that blacks are disproportionately imprisoned because of the war on drugs."[21]

The black inmate population reflects black criminality, not a racist criminal justice system, which currently is being run by one black man (Attorney General Holder) who reports to another (the president). Black crime rates are vastly higher than white crime rates. And it's hard to see how wishing away this reality, inventing conspiracy theories to explain it, or calling those who point it out "racist" will help improve the situation.

Perceptions of black criminality aren't likely to change until black behavior changes. Rather than address that challenge, however, too many liberal policy makers change the subject. Instead of talking about black behavior, they want to talk about racism or poverty or unemployment or gun control. The poverty argument is especially weak. In the 1950s, when segregation was legal, overt racism was rampant, and black poverty was much higher than today, black crime rates were lower and blacks comprised a smaller percentage of the prison population. And then there is the experience of other groups who endured rampant poverty, racial discrimination, and high unemployment without becoming overrepresented in the criminal justice system.

"During the 1960s, one neighborhood in San Francisco had the lowest income, the highest unemployment rate, the highest proportion of families with incomes under $4,000 per year, the least educational attainment, the highest tuberculosis rate, and the highest proportion of substandard housing in any area of the city," according to the social scientists Wilson and Herrnstein. "That neighborhood was called Chinatown. Yet in 1965, there were only five persons of Chinese ancestry committed to prison in the entire state of California."[22]

Those who want to blame crime on a lack of jobs cannot explain why crime rates fell in many cities during the Great Depression, when unemployment was high, and spiked during the 1960s, when economic growth was strong and jobs were plentiful. Indeed, the labor-force participation rate of young black men actually fell in the 1980s and 1990s, two of the longest periods of sustained economic growth in U.S. history. Shouldn't ghetto attitudes toward work at least be part of this discussion?

Gun control is another issue that the left raises to avoid discussing black behavior. After the Zimmerman verdict, Obama and Holder called for a reassessment of stand-your-ground laws, which allow people to use force to defend themselves without first retreating. "I know there's been commentary about the fact that stand-your-ground laws in Florida were not used as a defense of the case," said Obama. "On the other hand, if we're sending a message as a society in our communities that someone who is armed has a right to use those firearms even if there's a way for them to exit the situation, is that really going to be contributing to the kind of peace and security and order that we'd like to see?"

But do such laws, as the president and others have suggested, make us less safe? According to John Lott, a former chief economist at the United States Sentencing Commission, states with stand-your-ground laws (also known as castle doctrine laws) in place between 1977 and 2005 saw murder rates fall by 9 percent and overall violent crime fall by 11 percent.[23] "The debate has everything backwards over who benefits from the law," Lott told me in an e-mail exchange shortly after the Zimmerman verdict. "Poor blacks who live in high crime urban areas are not only the most likely victims of crime, they are also the ones who benefit the most from Stand Your Ground laws. It makes it easier for them to protect themselves when the police can't be there fast enough. Rules that make self-defense more difficult would impact blacks the most."

Lott noted that "blacks make up just 16.6 percent of Florida's population, but they account for over 31 percent of the state's defendants invoking Stand Your Ground defense. Black defendants who invoke this statute to justify their actions are acquitted 8 percent more frequently than whites who use the same defense." None of this is to suggest that there is a causal link between stand-your-ground laws and gun violence, though liberals like Obama seem certain that one exists. If they're right, it's an argument for more such laws, not fewer.

Gun deaths fell by 39 percent in the United States between 1993 and 2011. Justice Department data from 2013 show that "In less than two decades, the gun murder rate has been nearly cut in half. Other gun crimes fell even more sharply, paralleling a broader drop in violent crimes committed with or without guns."[24] More remarkable is that this drop in gun violence happened at the same time that firearm purchases were increasing. In 2012 background checks for gun purchases reached 19.6 million, an annual record, and an increase of 19 percent over 2011. Some of the most violent cities in America, like Chicago and Baltimore, already have some of the strictest gun laws. Yet the political left continues to insist that disarming ghetto residents improves safety in those communities.

Liberals like to obsess over how many people America incarcerates. They say that the number of inmates is simply "too high" or "excessive" without acknowledging the benefits of prison—benefits that accrue especially to the most likely crime victims: poor blacks. The relevant issue is not how many people we imprison per se but whether our higher arrests and conviction rates and longer prison terms affect behavior, wrote John Lott:

> *Many blacks have their lives disrupted by the criminal justice system, but the lives and property of many blacks are also protected by that same system. . . . Blacks overwhelmingly commit crime against other blacks. For example, in 2007, 90.2 percent of black murder victims were murdered by blacks. To go even further, poor blacks commit crime against poor blacks. Is it less racist to care about the victims or the criminals?*[25]

The reality is that locking up lawbreakers has worked better than going easy on them, and has worked best for law-abiding black people. After incarceration rates began to rise in the 1980s, crime plummeted. "The rate of reported crimes in the United States dropped each year after 1991 for nine years in a row, the longest decline ever recorded," wrote Franklin Zimring, a law professor at the University of California, Berkeley. "And crime dropped all over the United States—in every region, in the country as well as the city, in poor neighborhoods as well as rich neighborhoods. By the start of the twenty-first century, most serious crime rates had dropped by more than 35%."[26]

The homicide figures are particularly noteworthy. Between 1964 and 1974 the homicide rate more than doubled, and in the late 1980s was at 1974 levels. Then in the 1990s it fell consistently. "Even with more than 2,800 killings from the attack on September 11, 2001, the homicide rate that year was more than 30% lower than the periodic peak rates that were the top portions of the 20-year cycle that began in the mid-1970s,"[27] wrote Zimring. According to the Justice Department, the 1990s also saw declines of between 23 percent and 44 percent in rape, robbery, aggravated assault, burglary, auto theft, and larceny. Again, the benefits of less crime are not spread evenly throughout the population. Zimring explained:

> *The crime decline was the only public benefit of the 1990s whereby the poor and disadvantaged received more direct benefits than those with wealth. Because violent crime is a tax of which the poor pay much more, general crime declines also benefit the poor, as likely victims, most intensely. And impoverished minority males in big cities also benefited from less risk of both victimization and offense.*[28]

The professor added that the sharp decline in crime that big cities like New York, Dallas, Baltimore, Detroit, Los Angeles, Chicago, and Philadelphia experienced in the 1990s "could not have happened if crime was an inherent byproduct of urban disadvantage."[29]

For all the talk on the left that unemployment drives crime, the recent recession has not reversed trends. Between 2008 and 2010 the jobless rate doubled to about 10 percent, yet "the property-crime rate, far from spiking, fell significantly," according to the *Wall Street Journal*.

> *For 2009, the Federal Bureau of Investigation reported an 8% drop in the nationwide robbery rate and a 17% reduction in the auto-theft rate from the previous year. Big-city reports show the same thing. Between 2008 and 2010, New York City experienced a 4% decline in the robbery rate and a 10% fall in the burglary rate. Boston, Chicago and Los Angeles witnessed similar declines.*[30]

Factors other than incarceration rates can impact lawbreaking, of course. Criminologists agree that, for instance, the age structure of the population also matters, since young people commit more crimes. But there is no doubt that putting more people in prison for longer periods of time has contributed significantly to lowering crime rates in the United States. There is also no doubt that proactive policing and tough-on-crime policies that the left derides have led to fewer black deaths. In 2013 a federal judge in New York City declared the police department's use of stop and frisk unconstitutional, and appointed a monitor to reform the practice. The move was supported by Attorney General Holder. "To be clear, I'm not ordering an end to the practice of stop and frisk," wrote the judge, allowing that the Supreme Court has found the practice permissible. "The purpose of the remedies addressed in this opinion is to ensure that the practice is carried out in a manner that protects the rights and liberties of all New Yorkers, while still providing much-needed police protection." For the judge, however, as well as the ACLU, the NAACP, the Obama administration, and others on the left who cheered the ruling, the measure of whether a police stop is permissible is whether it comports with population data, not crime data. The judge didn't like the fact that blacks were stopped more often than whites and Asians. During the trial, police testified that they stopped people when they witnessed suspicious behavior and suspected criminal activity. They said that the disproportionate number of stops in black neighborhoods reflected the amount of crime in those neighborhoods, not anti-black bias. The judge was unpersuaded, ruling that police were conducting stops in a "racially discriminatory manner" that amounted to "indirect racial profiling."

It did not matter to critics that police cited stop and frisk as an important crime-fighting tool or that crime rates bore this out. Beginning in the 1960s, New York's murder rate rose steadily, peaking at 2,245 deaths in 1990. By 2012 the number had dropped to 419, a forty-year low. Former mayors Rudy Giuliani and Michael

Bloomberg and police commissioner Ray Kelly credited stop and frisk and other kinds of proactive policing as a major reason for the decline. Again, the biggest beneficiaries of this trend were blacks, who comprised 60 percent of murder victims in the Big Apple in 2012. "No police department in the country has come close to achieving what the NYPD has," wrote Heather Mac Donald. "New York's crime drop has been twice as deep and has lasted twice as long as the national average since the early 1990s. Today, 10,000 minority males are alive who would have been killed by now had New York's homicide rate remained at its early-1990s levels."[31] To the extent that soft-on-crime rulings like this result in less effective policing, blacks will suffer most.

The black civil rights leadership is fully aware that black criminality is, at root, a black problem that needs to be addressed by black people reassessing black behavior and cultural attitudes. But the civil rights movement has become an industry, and that industry has no vested interests in realistic assessments of black pathology. The NAACP responded to the Zimmerman verdict by announcing a series of national legislative initiatives. Ben Jealous, the head of the group at the time, said its goal was to "end racial profiling, repeal stand your ground laws, form effective civil complaint review boards to provide oversight of police misconduct, improve training for community watch groups, mandate law enforcement to collect data on homicide cases involving non-whites, and address the school to prison pipeline."[32] The NAACP, in other words, is way more interested in keeping whites on their toes than in addressing self-destructive black habits.

"The purpose of today's civil-rights establishment is not to seek justice, but to seek power for blacks in American life based on the presumption that they are still, in a thousand subtle ways, victimized by white racism," wrote Shelby Steele of the Hoover Institution in the aftermath of the Zimmerman verdict.

> *The civil-rights leadership rallied to Trayvon's cause (and not to the cause of those hundreds of black kids slain in America's inner cities this very year) to keep alive a certain cultural "truth" that is the sole source of the leadership's dwindling power. Put bluntly, this leadership rather easily tolerates black kids killing other black kids. But it cannot abide a white person (and Mr. Zimmerman, with his Hispanic background, was pushed into a white identity by the media over his objections) getting away with killing a black person without undermining the leadership's very reason for being.*[33]

In the days following the Zimmerman verdict, Bill O'Reilly used his Fox News program to call attention to "the disintegration of the African America family," which he identified as the ultimate source of "so much violence and chaos" in black communities. So long as 73 percent of black children are born to single mothers, said O'Reilly, blacks will find themselves overrepresented among delinquents. To his credit, Don Lemon, the black host of a program on CNN, applauded O'Reilly's remarks, and then added that O'Reilly "didn't go far enough." Lemon went on to make five simple suggestions for black self-improvement: pull up your pants, finish high school, stop using the n-word, take better care of your communities, and stop having children out of wedlock. The NAACP's agenda is about deflecting blame away from blacks and maintaining the relevance of the NAACP. Lemon's agenda is about personal responsibility. The social science, of course, overwhelmingly supports what both O'Reilly and Lemon are saying, even though many liberals want to ignore it and attack the messengers.

"The most critical factor affecting the prospect that a male youth will encounter the criminal justice system is the presence of his father in the home," concluded William Comanor and Llad Phillips after examining data from a national longitudinal study of young people. Black boys without a father were 68 percent more likely to be incarcerated than those with a father. James Q. Wilson put an even finer point on what's at stake:

> *If crime is to a significant degree caused by weak character; if weak character is more likely among the children of unmarried mothers; if there are no fathers who will help raise their children, acquire jobs, and protect their neighborhoods; if boys become young men with no preparation for work; if school achievement is regarded as a sign of having "sold out" to a dominant white culture; if powerful gangs replace weak families—if all these things are true, then the chances of reducing by plan and in the near future the crime rate of low-income blacks are slim.*[34]

The stark racial differences in crime rates undoubtedly impact black-white relations in America. So long as they persist, young black men will make people nervous. Discussions about the problem can be useful if they are honest, which is rare. Liberals don't help matters by making excuses for counterproductive behavior. Nor does the media by shying away from reporting the truth.

04

MANDATING UNEMPLOYMENT

The AFL-CIO is the nation's largest labor organization. A federation of fifty-six national and international unions representing more than twelve million workers, it was formed in 1955 when the American Federation of Labor joined with the Congress of Industrial Organizations. Since it typically backs Democratic presidential candidates, no one was especially surprised by the group's official endorsement of Barack Obama on June 26, 2008. What did cause something of a stir, however, was a speech given five days later at a steelworkers' convention in Las Vegas by the AFL-CIO's secretary-treasurer, Richard Trumka, who urged members not to stay home on Election Day just because Obama is black.

In his address, which later was posted on YouTube and garnered more than a half-million views (that's nothing if you're Beyoncé, but nothing to sneeze at if you're a gruff, middle-aged union boss), Trumka told of visiting his hometown of Nemacolin, Pennsylvania, just before the state's Democratic primary election and running into an elderly woman he had known as a child. When he asked the woman which candidate she was supporting, she said Hillary Clinton. Trumka asked her why, and the woman, after some coaxing, eventually said that it was due to Obama's race. "There's a lot of folks out there just like that woman, and a lot of them are good union people," says Trumka in the video, assuring everyone that dues-paying bigots are welcome in the labor movement. "They just can't get past the idea that there is something wrong with voting for a black man. Well, those of us who know better can't afford to sit silently or look the other way while it's happening."

"There is no evil that has inflicted more pain and more suffering than racism," continues Trumka, who would become president of the AFL-CIO the following year. "And it's something that we in the labor movement have a very, very special responsibility to challenge."

Watching the video, I perked up at this point, curious where Trumka might be headed. Union leaders may be dismayed by remnants of overt racism in the rank and file, but it's hardly surprising, given the history of the American labor movement. As Paul Moreno, the author of *Black Americans and Organized Labor*, noted, "Organized labor was largely hostile to the antislavery movement, and most abolitionists opposed unions." Moreno wrote that "white workers feared competition from emancipated slaves, and white workers in the North especially feared an influx of southern freedmen."[1]

After the Civil War black leaders continued to be skeptical of unions. In his 1874 essay "The Folly, Tyranny, and Wickedness of

Labor Unions," Frederick Douglass argued that there was "abundant proof almost every day of their mischievous influence upon every industrial interest in the country." W. E. B. Du Bois called trade unions "the greatest enemy of the black working man." Booker T. Washington, who was born a slave and opposed unions his entire life, wrote in the *Atlantic Monthly* in 1913 that "the average Negro who comes to town does not understand the necessity or advantage of a labor organization which stands between him and his employer and aims apparently to make a monopoly of the opportunity for labor."

It was Washington's view that for all of the suffering endured under slavery, that institution had left blacks with many of the skills necessary to rise economically—"not only as farmers but as carpenters, blacksmiths, wheelwrights, brick masons, engineers"—if only unions would let them. T. Thomas Fortune, a leading black journalist and Washington confidant, expressed a similar sentiment in a 1903 essay. "In the skilled trades, at the close of the War of the Rebellion, most of the work was done by Negroes educated as artisans in the hard school of slavery," wrote Fortune, who like Washington was born a slave. "But there has been a steady decline in the number of such laborers, not because of lack of skill, but because trade unionism has gradually taken possession of such employments in the South, and will not allow the Negro to work alongside of the white man. And this is the rule of the trade unions in all parts of the country."

Economist Ray Marshall, President Jimmy Carter's pro-union labor secretary, made a name for himself in academia by documenting how labor unions have discriminated against blacks. In his 1967 book, *The Negro Worker*, which includes a chapter titled "The Racial Practices of National and Local Unions," Marshall wrote that "in 1930 there were at least 26 national unions which barred Negroes from membership by formal means," and ten of them were AFL affiliates. After the Supreme Court's 1954 school desegregation ruling, anti-integrationist unions formed, and actively recruited members of the Ku Klux Klan. Official policies toward black workers began to change when the AFL merged with the CIO, which was more committed to racial equality, but Marshall cautioned:

> *The decline in formal exclusion by international unions does not mean that discrimination has declined, because local affiliates of these unions, as well as others which never had formal race bars, exclude Negroes by a number of informal means. These include agreements not to sponsor Negroes for membership; refusal to admit Negroes into apprenticeship programs or to accept their applications; general "understandings" to vote against Negroes if they are proposed . . . [and] refusal of journeyman status to Negroes by means of examinations which either are not given to whites or are rigged so that Negroes cannot pass them.*[2]

This history is not well known today. And unlike their predecessors, the contemporary black elite tend to argue that the interests of Big Labor and the black underclass are more or less aligned. Labor unions give generously to black organizations like the NAACP, the National Urban League, Jesse Jackson's Rainbow PUSH Coalition, and Al Sharpton's National Action Network. In return, black leaders parrot the union line. But when Trumka told his audience that the labor movement has a "special responsibility" to challenge racism, I thought for a moment that he was about to pay some lip service to this ugly past.

Silly me.

It turned out that the reason Big Labor has a unique obligation to confront racism has nothing at all to do with the movement's own history of discrimination. Rather, it's because unions "know, better than anyone else, how racism is used to divide working people," Trumka said. "We've seen how companies set worker against worker. They throw white workers a few crumbs. They discriminate against black workers or Latino workers. And we all—we all—end up losing." In Trumka's telling, the labor movement has been a force for racial equality, and the real enemy of blacks is corporate America. As for that Hillary Clinton supporter he encountered? "I don't think we ought to be out there pointing fingers and calling them racists," he said. "Instead we need to educate them."

Trumka did not educate his audience that day with any examples of how corporate racism has been more detrimental to blacks than the union variety, maybe because there is so little evidence pointing in that direction. Yet there is plenty of evidence that many public policies supported by the AFL-CIO and other labor groups today leave the black underclass worse off. The problem is not that today's labor leaders are motivated by racial animus. Rather, it's that so much of what they advocate in the name of expanding the middle class is in practice preventing many blacks from joining its ranks.

Minimum-wage laws, which determine the lowest price for labor that an employer may pay, are one of the more obvious examples of this phenomenon. But to understand why these laws make it harder for blacks to find jobs, it first helps to look at how minimum-wage laws impact labor markets in general. And it turns out that economists, a famously argumentative lot, tend to agree that minimum-wage laws destroy jobs. In fact, polls have shown that more than

90 percent of professional economists contend that increasing the minimum wage lowers employment for minimum-wage workers. Even highly respected economists such as David Card and Alan Krueger, who are skeptical of the consensus view, concede that the minimum-wage hypothesis "is one of the clearest and most widely appreciated in the field of economics."[3] Why? Because a basic tenet of economics is that a rise in the cost of something tends to lower demand for it. Put another way, an artificial increase in the price of something causes less of it to be purchased. When that something is the price of labor, the result is a labor surplus, also known as unemployment. "It's simple," wrote Gary Becker, who won the Nobel Prize in Economics in 1992, "hike the minimum wage and you put people out of work."[4]

In 2008 economists David Neumark and William Wascher published a book that surveyed the minimum-wage literature of the previous three decades. They reviewed more than one hundred academic studies on the impact of such laws and found "overwhelming" evidence that younger, lesser-skilled workers suffer what economists call "disemployment effects," or a loss of employment when the minimum wage goes up:

> *Our overall sense of the literature is that the preponderance of evidence supports the view that minimum wages reduce the employment of low-wage workers. . . . Moreover, when researchers focus on the least-skilled groups that are most likely to be directly affected by minimum wage increases, the evidence for disemployment effects seems especially strong."*[5]

When the government mandates that an employer pay someone more than the employer thinks the person is worth, fewer people get hired.

When I asked Neumark, a professor of economics at the University of California, Irvine, about research that shows no harmful effects on hiring when the minimum wage is increased, he told me that those studies are outliers. "There's quite a bit of agreement," he said in an interview. "You do see papers sometimes claiming that there are no disemployment effects from the minimum wage. They tend to come from the same people. And clearly some of them, the ones coming out of the UC Berkeley group"—a reference to the famously liberal flagship campus of the University of California—"clearly they have a political agenda." Neumark also said that the press has a tendency to play up contrarian studies, which gives them more weight than they might deserve. "Most of the studies say there's a disemployment effect, so that's not really news anymore. So you get disproportionate attention in the media and sometimes in the profession to studies that find surprising results."[6]

Two go-to academics for the pro-minimum-wage crowd are the aforementioned David Card of Berkeley and Alan Krueger of Princeton. In 1994, when both men were teaching at Princeton, they coauthored a widely cited case study that compared employment changes in fast-food restaurants in New Jersey and Pennsylvania after New Jersey's minimum wage rose from $4.25 to $5.05 per hour. Following the increase employment fell in New Jersey, as most economists would have predicted. But because it also fell by just as much in Pennsylvania, which hadn't hiked its own minimum, Card and Krueger argued that the drop in both states must have been caused by something else. "Contrary to the central prediction of the textbook model of the minimum wage," the authors concluded, "we find no evidence that the rise in New Jersey's minimum wage reduced employment at fast-food restaurants in the state."

In their subsequent book, *Myth and Measurement: The New Economics of the Minimum Wage*, the authors went even further.

Under close scrutiny, the bulk of the empirical evidence on the employment effects of the minimum wage is shown to be consistent with our findings . . . which suggest that increases in the minimum wage have had, if anything, a small, positive effect on employment, rather than an adverse effect.[7]

But others immediately pushed back at that notion, and quite hard. Becker wrote that the Card and Krueger studies had "serious defects," and other economists—including Donald Deere, Finis Welch, and Kevin Murphy—spelled them out in detail. A major flaw, it turned out, was the shortness of the sample periods used in the case studies, which didn't allow enough time for the negative employment effects to show up. "Subsequent research has tended to confirm evidence of adverse longer-run effects of minimum wages on employment," explained Neumark and Wascher. Similarly, a 1997 study from the union-backed Employment Policy Institute claimed that employment didn't decline after a 1996 increase in the federal minimum wage. But later studies showed that EPI obtained that result by using just six months of data. Adding three more months of data would have reversed the conclusion:

The research on this issue suggests that studies claiming to find no minimum wage effect on employment should be discounted unless the evidence points to no effects in both the short run and the longer run. Indeed, this issue turns out to figure prominently in our assessment of the research literature, as the studies that fail to detect disemployment effects typically do not allow for a longer-run impact.[8]

The preponderance of evidence continues to show, as it has for decades, that minimum-wage laws tend to lead to overall job loss, which is bad enough. But the most insidious aspect of these policies is that the job loss is concentrated among the least-educated and least-skilled workers—the same group that minimum-wage advocates are trying to help. And blacks, it so happens, are overrepresented in this segment of the population. According to 2011 Census Bureau data, the median age for blacks in the United States is 31, versus 37.3 for all Americans. The black population is growing faster than the total population—it grew by 15 percent between 2000 and 2010, compared with growth of 9.7 percent among all groups over the same period—and the young black population is growing especially fast. The Census Bureau projects that the number of black persons under age 18 will grow by 5 percent between 2015 and 2025, "while white, non-Hispanic juveniles will decrease by 4%."[9]

Blacks are also more likely than the general public to be living in poverty—28.1 percent versus 15.9 percent—and their median household income of $33,460 significantly trails the national median of $50,502.[10] When it comes to educational achievement, the gap between blacks and whites is especially pronounced. A 2010 Schott Foundation for Public Education survey of all fifty states concluded that just 47 percent of black males complete high school. In some major cities like New York and Philadelphia, that rate is 20 percentage points lower. Blacks who do proceed to college are also much less likely than whites to graduate. A 2012 article in the *Journal of Blacks in Higher Education*, citing U.S. Department of Education figures, noted that among students who entered college in 2005 and earned their degree within six years the graduation rate was 60.2 percent for whites and 37.9 percent for blacks, a 22-point difference.[11]

Minimum-wage mandates don't impact all workers equally, but they are especially harmful to those who are young and those who are living on the margins, where many blacks for various reasons find themselves. What such individuals want and need are job opportunities, which minimum-wage laws reduce by pricing people out of the labor market. These laws keep the large number of blacks who lack the right education and skills from being able to compete for jobs by offering to work for less money, get on-the-job experience, and ultimately increase their skills and pay. Alan Greenspan, the former chairman of the Federal Reserve, told a congressional hearing in 2001 that he would abolish the minimum wage if he could. "I'm not in favor of cutting anybody's earnings or preventing them from rising," he said, "but I am against them losing their jobs because of artificial government intervention, which is essentially what the minimum wage is."[12]

The well-meaning liberals who defend these laws today ignore their racial impact, but it is undeniable that race was on the minds of those who initially championed a federal wage floor. States took the lead in establishing a minimum wage, with Massachusetts going first in 1912. Within a decade, fifteen states and the District of Columbia had minimum-wage laws on their books. This was the Progressive Era, and proponents said that workers were being exploited and needed more bargaining power. Employers disagreed, and challenged the laws in court on the grounds that they "violated employers' constitutional rights to enter freely into contracts and deprived them of their private property (i.e., their profits) without due process," wrote economists Neumark and Wascher.[13] The Supreme Court agreed in a 1923 ruling against the District of Columbia's minimum-wage law. And by the end of the decade similar laws in most other places had been declared unconstitutional, repealed, or otherwise neutered to avoid a legal challenge. They would reappear in 1933, when President Franklin D. Roosevelt signed the National Industrial Recovery Act, which called for workweeks of thirty-five to forty hours and minimum pay of $12 to $15 per week. The Supreme Court would find that unconstitutional as well in 1935, but not before an estimated half a million black workers lost their jobs due to the minimum-wage requirements.

"Blacks were major victims of the NRA [the National Recovery Administration]. The labor codes were drawn up by craft unions that excluded blacks as members and did everything they could to promote the interests of white workers and to subvert the interests of blacks, who were seen as competition," wrote Jim Powell in *FDR's Folly.* "Moreover, by sanctioning compulsory unionism, the NRA labor codes effectively excluded blacks from many jobs."

There were an estimated 2.25 million union workers in 1933, and only about 2 percent were black. "Daily the problem of what to do about union labor or even about a chance to work, confronts the Negro workers of the country," said the NAACP publication the *Crisis* in November 1934. "Union labor strategy seems to be to form a union in a given plant, strike to obtain the right to bargain with the employees as the sole representative of labor, and then to close the union to black workers, effectively cutting them off from employment."[14]

But the Supreme Court would not have the last word. Three years later, at the urging of unions, Congress would establish a federal minimum wage with the Fair Labor Standards Act of 1938. As former Labor Department economist Morgan Reynolds explained,

During the confusion of the Great Depression, Congress supplied six major pieces of labor legislation favored by unionists: Davis-Bacon, Norris-La Guardia, National Industrial Recovery Act, National Labor Relations (Wagner) Act, Walsh-Healey, and Fair Labor Standards Act. Three of the bills (Davis-Bacon,

Walsh-Healey, and Fair Labor) authorized direct federal regula-
tion of wages, hours, and working conditions in various sectors
of the economy.[15]

The Norris-La Guardia and Wagner acts would make it unlawful
for an employer to discriminate against a worker for belonging to
a union. Walsh-Healey allowed the secretary of labor to determine
minimum-wage scales for nearly all government contractors, but a
1964 court decision rendered it inoperable on due process grounds.
However, the Fair Labor Standards Act and the Davis-Bacon Act,
which was passed in 1931, remain in force today and continue to
destroy jobs for millions of people, many of them black. This is
not an accident. It was the intent.

The express purpose of Davis-Bacon is to protect the wages and
employment of union workers in the buildings trades. Under the
law, which is really just a super-minimum wage for the construction industry, workers on federally funded construction projects
must be paid wages at "prevailing" rates. "The methodology used
to calculate this prevailing wage sets it close to union wage scales
and well above average wages," explained the Heritage Foundation
in a 2007 report. "Davis-Bacon rates are typically 15 to 40 percent
higher than average wages for the same job. In some cases, Davis-
Bacon rates more than double the competitive wage." In Nassau
and Suffolk counties on New York's Long Island, for example,
Davis-Bacon required a minimum wage for brickmasons of $49.67
per hour, according to a 2008 *Wall Street Journal* editorial, "though
the more common area wage for that work is $22.50."

That the law discriminates against nonunion contractors and in
the process inflates the cost of federal projects for taxpayers should
be reason enough to scrap it, especially at a time when the government is running trillion-dollar deficits. But blacks have long had

a separate legitimate gripe with Davis-Bacon because most black construction workers today, just like in the 1930s, aren't unionized. "Democrats support these blanket Davis-Bacon policies even though minorities are still victimized by the wage law," reported the *Journal*. "A 2001 study by economists Daniel Kessler of Stanford and Lawrence Katz of Harvard found that when states have repealed their Davis-Bacon laws, this 'is associated with a decline in the union wage premium and an appreciable narrowing of the black/nonblack wage differential for construction workers.'"[16] In fact, Davis-Bacon has been so effective at putting blacks out of work that 1930, the year before the law passed, was the last year that the black jobless rate was lower than the white rate.[17]

"While blacks were excluded from most major construction unions, they were nonetheless a formidable force in the construction industry," noted economist Walter Williams of George Mason University, who has written extensively about blacks and labor law.

> *In 1930, the industry in the South provided more jobs to blacks than any other except agriculture and domestic services. In six Southern cities, blacks represented more than 80 percent of the unskilled labor force. . . . During this period, significant demographic changes were taking place. Blacks were increasingly migrating northward and establishing a foothold in the Northern construction workforce.*[18]

We don't need to guess what politicians were thinking when they moved to implement federal minimum-wage laws and Davis-Bacon statutes. We still have the transcripts of what was actually said by proponents. And it's crystal clear that Congress passed these statutes to protect white union workers from competition from nonunion blacks. As with the minimum wage, states took the lead in implementing prevailing-wage laws. Kansas went first in 1891, and New York followed three years later. Both efforts were the brainchild of American Federation of Labor president Samuel Gompers. The push at the federal level started in 1927, when a contractor from Alabama won a bid to construct a Veteran's Bureau hospital on Long Island and brought black workers from the South to complete the job. Because it was a federal contract, New York's prevailing-wage law didn't apply. Congressman Robert Bacon, who represented the district where the hospital was located, received complaints from constituents that contractors were bidding wages down and displacing local workers. The following year Bacon introduced federal legislation that would require contractors working on federal public works projects to comply with states' prevailing-wage laws. It would ultimately be cosponsored by Senator James Davis of Pennsylvania and go through numerous iterations before finally becoming law in 1931.

During hearings, Representative William Upshaw of Georgia sympathized with Bacon, noting "the real problem that you are confronted with in any community with a superabundance or large aggregation of negro labor." Missouri Representative John Cochran, another supporter, said that he had "received numerous complaints in recent months about Southern contractors employing low-paid colored mechanics getting work and bringing the employees from the South." Alabama Representative Miles Allgood recounted the story of "a contractor from Alabama who went to New York with bootleg labor. This is a fact. That contractor has cheap colored labor that he transports, and he puts them in cabins, and it is labor of that sort that is in competition with white labor throughout the country."

Nor did organized labor stand by idly while the national Davis-Bacon debate raged. "Testimony by union representatives reveals a

definite racial element to their support," wrote David Bernstein in
Only One Place of Redress, a history of blacks and labor regulations.

> *William J. Spencer, secretary of the buildings-trades depart-*
> *ment of the American Federation of Labor, told the committee,*
> *"There are complaints from all hospitals of the Veteran's Bureau*
> *against the condition of employment on these jobs. That is true*
> *whether the job is the States of Washington, Oregon, Oklahoma,*
> *or Florida. The same complaints come in. They are due to the*
> *fact that a contractor from Alabama may go to North Port*
> *and take a crew of negro workers and house them on the site*
> *of construction within a stockade and feed them and keep his*
> *organization intact thereby and work that job contrary to the*
> *existing practices in the city of New York."*[19]

The debates over the federal minimum wage are no less
revealing. Since the Fair Labor Standards Act passed in 1938, Congress has amended it repeatedly to increase the legal minimum and
extend its coverage. "The loss in jobs caused by the minimum wage
is not an accidental byproduct of higher minimum wages. It is the
consequence intended by those who most avidly support increasing
minimum wages," explained economist David Henderson in his
2002 book, *The Joy of Freedom*.

> *Northern unions and unionized firms, for example, have tra-*
> *ditionally supported higher minimum wages to hobble their*
> *low-wage competition in the South. . . . Forty years ago, the*
> *politicians who pushed for the increased minimum wage did*
> *not hide their motives. Nor, in an era of state-sanctioned seg-*
> *regation, did they feel the need to hide their knowledge of who*
> *the intended victims of minimum-wage increases would be.*

Here is Senator John F. Kennedy of Massachusetts, who supported increasing the minimum wage, addressing an NAACP official at a Senate hearing in 1957:

Of course, having on the market a rather large source of cheap labor depresses wages outside of that group, too—the wages of the white worker who has to compete. And when an employer can substitute a colored worker at a lower wage—and there are, as you pointed out, these hundreds of thousands looking for decent work—it affects the whole wage structure of an area, doesn't it?

Roughly a decade later, in 1966, Senator Jacob Javits of New York would make a strikingly similar argument in favor of raising the federal minimum. "I point out to Senators from industrial states like my own that a minimum wage increase would also give industry in our states some measure of protection," said Javits, "as we have too long suffered from the unfair competition based on substandard wages and other labor conditions in effect in certain areas of the country—primarily in the South."[20]

Yes, sometimes a government policy has consequences that are not intended or anticipated. But minimum-wage laws are not an example of such. The issue today is not whether proponents of the minimum wage are motivated by the same racial animus that characterized earlier proponents. The issue is whether these wage mandates continue to harm blacks disproportionately, regardless of intent. For decades the black unemployment rate has tended to be about double that of whites, irrespective of the economic climate. At the end of 2012 jobless rates were 6.3 percent for whites, 9.8 percent for Hispanics, and 14 percent for blacks. Even during periods of strong economic growth such as the 1990s the labor participation rate for black men between 16 and 24 fell.

Black leaders today continue to cite racism as a major cause of black unemployment (and every other socioeconomic problem that blacks face). Yet in 1930, when racial discrimination was infinitely more open and rampant, the black unemployment rate was lower than that of whites. And until around 1950 the unemployment rate for young black men was much lower than today, and similar to whites in the same age group. "Black 16-year-olds and 17-year-olds had a slightly lower unemployment rate than white youngsters of the same age in 1948 and only slightly higher unemployment rates than their white peers in 1949," wrote Stanford economist Thomas Sowell. How come? Sowell offered one plausible explanation:

> This was just before the minimum wage law was amended in 1950 to catch up with the inflation of the 1940s which had, for all practical purposes, repealed the minimum wage law, since inflated wages for even unskilled labor were usually well above the minimum wage level specified when the Fair Labor Standards Act was passed in 1938.
>
> The key role of the federal minimum wage laws can be seen in the fact that black teenage unemployment, even in the recession year of 1949, was a fraction of what it would become in even prosperous later years, after the series of minimum wage escalations that began in 1950.[21]

So while racism may not drive today's proponents of minimum-wage laws, the effects of these laws continue to disproportionately harm the job opportunities of blacks in general, and young blacks in particular. Nevertheless black politicians, civil rights groups, and their liberal allies continue to ignore the empirical data and back these disastrous policies. In May of 2011 the Chicago Urban League, a civil rights group that supports minimum-wage laws, released a study of youth employment prepared by Northeastern University's Center for Labor Market Studies. The study found that despite overall job growth in the previous year, "the nation's teenagers did not manage to capture any of the increase in employment." Indeed, 2010 was "the fifth consecutive year in which a new historical low for teen employment was reached," and the center predicted that "only one of every four teens (16–19 years old) would be employed during the summer months of June, July, and August," which would represent the "lowest ever or second lowest ever summer employment rate for teens in post-WWII history." When the study was released, the national unemployment rate was 9.1 percent, but it was 24.2 percent for teens, and 40.7 percent for black teens. In Chicago the situation was much worse, said the Urban League, noting that "90 percent [of black teens] are jobless, including 93 of every 100 teens from families with incomes under $40,000; upper-middle-income whites were nearly four times as likely to hold a job, the data show."

The report went on to lament that "this national disaster has not received any substantive attention from the nation's economic policymakers of either political party." But that wasn't quite true. A separate study, released around the same time by labor economists William Even of Miami University in Ohio and David Macpherson of Trinity University in Texas, detailed how recent federal minimum-wage hikes had in fact contributed to this "national disaster." Congress had raised the federal minimum by 41 percent, to $7.25 an hour, in three stages between 2007 and 2009. The problem was not indifference, but that policy makers had made matters worse.

The Even and Macpherson study found that for white males ages 16 to 24, each 10 percent increase in a federal or state minimum wage had decreased employment by 2.5 percent. For Hispanic males the figure was 1.2 percent. "But among black males in this group,

each 10% increase in the minimum wage has decreased employment by 6.5%." The effect on black workers was so pronounced,
wrote the authors, that "employment losses for 16-to-24-year-old
black males between 2007 and 2010 could have been nearly 50%
lower had the federal and state minimum wages remained at the
January 2007 level."

And as you dug into the numbers, the story got even worse.
Not all states were impacted equally by the federal minimum-
wage increases, because some already mandated a minimum wage
above the federal requirement. But in the twenty-one states that
were fully affected, 13,200 young blacks lost their jobs as a direct
result of the recession, versus 18,500 who lost their jobs as a result
of the minimum-wage mandates. "In other words," wrote Even
and Macpherson, "the consequences of the minimum wage for
this subgroup were more harmful than the consequences of the
recession."[22]

The irony is that the same liberals who complain about the
dearth of employment opportunities in the ghetto—from President
Obama to the Congressional Black Caucus to black mayors and
MSNBC talking heads—are among the loudest defenders of the
minimum wage. In his first State of the Union address after being
reelected, Obama called for increasing the federal minimum by 24
percent, from $7.25 to $9 an hour, and indexing it to inflation. At
the time of the speech in February 2013, unemployment was 7.9
percent overall, but 13.8 percent among blacks (versus 7 percent
among whites), 14.5 percent among black men (versus 7.2 percent
among white men), and 37.8 percent among black teens (versus
20.8 percent among white teens).

In separate interviews, Professors Macpherson and Even told
me that several factors contribute to the racial disparities resulting
from minimum-wage hikes. "One problem is that I think blacks

tend to have, on average, inferior schooling," Macpherson said. "Also, the effects of the minimum wage differ by industry, and blacks tend to be heavily concentrated in, for example, eating and drinking establishments, where it's easier to substitute capital for labor." Geography also plays a role, said Even. "Fifty-seven percent of blacks [between 16 and 24] are in the South. Only a third of whites are. And only a third of Hispanics are." He added: "The South generally has had lower wages than other parts of the country. And so a minimum of $7.25 is likely to be more binding, or affect more people in the South, than it will in other regions. So when you have these federal policies where one size fits all, and a disproportionate share of blacks live in areas where the minimum wage hits hardest, this could be part of the explanation of what's going on."

The reality is that as the minimum wage has risen, the gap between the overall jobless rate and the jobless rate of young people has widened. This holds true at the federal and state level. "At least 10 states have raised their minimum wages above the federal level in the last decade, largely in response to union lobbying," reported the *Wall Street Journal* in 2009. "Four states with among the highest wage rates are California, Massachusetts, Michigan and New York. Studies have shown in each case that their wage policies killed jobs for teens." This phenomenon extends beyond U.S. borders, by the way. A study of seventeen other countries found a "highly negative association between higher minimum wages and youth employment rates," said the *Journal*. "It also concluded that having a starter wage, well below the minimum, counteracts much of this negative jobs impact."

Minimum-wage defenders don't have much in the way of hard data to refute the disemployment effects of these policies. Instead, they argue that minimum-wage laws alleviate poverty, which is the greater good, in their view. Here's how Obama put it in his 2013 State of the Union address:

> We know our economy is stronger when we reward an honest day's work with honest wages. But today, a full-time worker making the minimum wage earns $14,500 a year. Even with the tax relief we put in place, a family with two kids that earns the minimum wage still lives below the poverty line. That's wrong. That's why, since the last time this Congress raised the minimum wage, nineteen states have chosen to bump theirs even higher.
>
> Tonight, let's declare that in the wealthiest nation on Earth, no one who works full-time should have to live in poverty, and raise the federal minimum wage to $9.00 an hour. . . . This single step would raise the incomes of millions of working families. It could mean the difference between groceries or the food bank; rent or eviction; scraping by or finally getting ahead. For businesses across the country, it would mean customers with more money in their pockets.

The belief that minimum-wage laws are an effective antipoverty tool has a long pedigree on the political left. "Without question," said President Roosevelt in 1938 after Congress passed the federal minimum, "it starts us toward a better standard of living and increases purchasing power to buy the products of farm and factory." Sixty years later President Clinton would say at a press conference that upping the minimum wage would "raise the living standards of twelve million hard-working Americans." Senator Ted Kennedy would declare that "the minimum wage was one of the first—and is still one of the best—antipoverty programs we have." And Clinton labor secretary Robert Reich told Congress in 1995 that the federal minimum was "just not enough to support a family" and that "a moderate increase in the minimum wage is one of the few steps that government can take to improve the living standards of low-income workers."[23] After the minimum wage rose in 2009, Obama labor secretary Hilda Solis announced that millions of Americans were now "a step closer to making ends meet every month."

The minimum wage has increased during Democratic and Republican administrations alike, though Republicans have tended to approve hikes reluctantly, and usually in return for something else to help offset the damage, like tax breaks for small businesses. And it's true that a minimum-wage hike will improve the lot of those making the minimum, provided they keep their jobs and continue to work the same number of hours, neither of which should be assumed. Remember that minimum wages deal with wages, not employment. The government can mandate that someone be paid at a level above his productivity, but it can't (yet) mandate that he be hired in the first place, or that he keep his job after the cost of employing him rises. So some people will lose their job or never be hired, and others will get a raise. But on balance, are low-skill workers better off?

You can begin to answer that question by looking at who's earning the minimum wage. And when you do, you realize how dishonest it is when proponents depict the typical minimum-wage beneficiary as someone who is poor or a household head. In reality the typical minimum-wage earner is neither. "It's always the low-income families that policy makers say they want to help, and with good reason," economist David Neumark told me in an interview. "But my reading of the evidence"—and he has studied as much of the literature as anyone—"is that there is zero compelling evidence that minimum-wage increases have beneficial distributional effects, that they're helping people at the bottom. And there's some hint that there are some negative effects." Neumark said that "roughly speaking, over the past twenty years a third of minimum-wage workers are in families in the top half of the income distribution. The median income for a family of four is between fifty and sixty thousand dollars. Minimum-wage workers are not in poor families. They're not even in families that are twice the poverty line. If you're 30 and earning minimum wage, you're probably in a poor family. But if you're 17 and earning minimum wage, you're more likely not to be in a poor family, because 17-year-olds in poor families probably aren't working." Thanks in part to the minimum wage.

"One of the reasons the minimum wage really misses the mark and doesn't do much for poor people is that it targets the poor really badly," said Neumark. "The only targeting you're doing with the minimum wage is targeting people based on wages. And the mapping between a low-wage worker and a low-income family is very fuzzy and very loose." He was echoing a sentiment expressed by Nobel economist George Stigler in 1946. "The connection between hourly wages and the standard of living of the family is remote and fuzzy," wrote Stigler. "Unless the minimum wage varies with the amount of employment, number of earners, nonwage income, family size, and many other factors, it will be an inept device for combating poverty even for those who succeed in retaining employment."

Around 5 percent of hourly workers in the United States earn the minimum wage, according to the 2012 data from the Bureau of Labor Statistics and the Census Bureau. Most are 25 or younger and 69 percent of them work part-time. They are not their families' sole breadwinner; they come from households that don't depend on their earnings. Thus, the beneficiary of a minimum-wage increase is more likely to be a teenager in a tony suburb than a single mom in the ghetto. And hiking the minimum wage will diminish the job prospects for that single mom. A 1995 study concluded that mothers in states that raised the minimum wage remained on public assistance an average of 44 percent longer than their peers in states where the minimum did not rise.

If anything, minimum-wage policies have become less and less effective over time as an antipoverty tool, according to Cornell University economists Richard Burkhauser and Joseph Sabia. In 1939, the year the federal minimum was established, 94 percent of household heads who were low-wage workers were in poor families, along with 85 percent of all low-wage workers. By 1969 those figures were 45 percent and 23 percent, respectively. By 2003 they were 11 percent and 9 percent.

"We find no evidence that minimum wage increases between 2003 and 2007 lowered state poverty rates. Moreover, we find that the newly proposed federal minimum wage increase from $7.25 to $9.50 per hour, like the last increase from $5.15 to $7.25 per hour, is not well targeted to the working poor," wrote Burkhauser and Sabia in a 2010 paper.

> *Only 11.3% of workers who will gain from an increase in the federal minimum wage to $9.50 per hour live in poor households, an even smaller share than was the case with the last federal minimum wage increase (15.8%). Of those who will gain, 63.2% are second or third earners living in households with incomes twice the poverty line, and 42.3% live in households with incomes three times the poverty line, well above $50,233, the income of the median household in 2007.*

Liberals bleat on about raising the federal floor to help the working poor, but most poor people already make more than the minimum, and most people who earn the minimum wage aren't poor.

With all due respect to the late Ted Kennedy, the best antipoverty program is not the minimum wage. Rather, it's a job, even if it's an entry-level one. Most poor families don't have *any* workers. Raising the minimum wage does nothing for them, and to the extent that it reduces their employment opportunities, it's a net negative. Reducing the number of entry-level jobs keeps people poor by limiting their ability to enter or remain in the workforce, where they have the opportunity to obtain the skills necessary to increase their productivity and pay, and ultimately improve their lives.

Unions support minimum wages not because they want to help the working poor but because they want to protect their members, who already have jobs. "Just as businesses seek to have government impose tariffs on imported goods that compete with their products, so labor unions use minimum wage laws as tariffs to force up the price of non-union labor that competes with their members for jobs," wrote Thomas Sowell in *Basic Economics*.[24] What's painful is watching black leaders align themselves with unions that are working against the interests of low-income blacks who are out of work. Walmart, for example, has a history of locating its stores in less affluent neighborhoods and providing those residents with not only jobs but low-cost goods and services. The political left claims to care so much more than conservatives about the well-being of the poor. But labor unions and Democratic politicians from Obama on down would rather have these ghetto residents stay poor and jobless if the alternative is allowing them to work at a Walmart that won't bow to union demands. In 2012, after Walmart announced that it had dropped plans to construct a big-box store in an economically depressed section of New York City, labor leaders and liberal activists cheered. "Walmart's withdrawal," said Stephanie Yazgi of Walmart Free NYC, "shows that when New Yorkers join arms, even the world's richest retailer is no match for them." It also showed that the actual needs of the underprivileged take a back seat to the left's political agenda.

05

EDUCATIONAL
FREEDOM

One of the more worrisome trends in K–12 education is the achievement gap between black and white students in America, which has persisted for decades despite massive injections of money and resources. Federal per-pupil spending rose by an inflation-adjusted 375 percent between 1970 and 2010. School spending also grew steadily and dramatically at the state and local level, tripling between 1970 and 2005. Over the decades the government has prioritized poor children through programs such as Title I, which was created in 1965. "These federal streams accomplished precisely what was intended: helping equalize the funding of poor and affluent districts," explained education writer Andy Smarick. "As of the 2004–5 school year, America's highest-poverty districts had per student revenues virtually equivalent to the nation's lowest-poverty districts."[1]

Notwithstanding this increase in overall education spending—and dogged efforts to ensure that inner-city schools aren't financially neglected—test scores in math, science, and reading have remained essentially flat for forty years. Moreover, significant racial disparities in outcomes continue. The learning gap between blacks and whites, as measured by national-average test scores, narrowed somewhat through most of the 1980s, but began to widen toward the end of that decade, and ultimately returned to where it had been in the late 1970s. In 2004, black 9-year-olds trailed their white peers in reading by roughly the same amount that they had twenty-five years earlier.[2] Black 17-year-olds scored at the same level in reading and math as white 13-year-olds. And white 13-year-olds outperformed black 17-year-olds in science. In five out of seven categories—math, science, history, physics, and geography—a majority of blacks scored at the lowest level.[3]

On average, black fourth and eighth graders perform two full grade levels behind their white peers.[4] Large urban school districts where a majority of children are black or Hispanic produce even worse results. A U.S. Department of Education report released in 2012 showed that 79 percent of eighth graders in Chicago public schools, which are 41 percent black and 44 percent Hispanic, could not read at grade level, and 80 percent could not perform grade-level math. Incredibly, those students were still better off than their peers in Detroit, where 7 percent of eighth graders were proficient in reading and only 4 percent were proficient in math.[5] Detroit public schools, which are 95 percent black, "had the lowest scores ever recorded in the 21-year history of the national math proficiency test" in 2009, reported the *New York Times*.[6]

The crisis is most pronounced among young black males, and even transcends socioeconomic status, asserted David Kirp, a professor of public policy at the University of California, Berkeley. "On every measure of educational attainment, they [black boys] fare the worst; despite waves of reform, their situation has not changed appreciably in 30 years," he wrote.

> *The gap between their performance and that of their peers is perceptible from the first day of kindergarten, and only widens thereafter. In the 2008 National Assessment of Educational Progress—the massive, federally mandated report card on student performance, measured in grades 4, 8, and 12—the reading scores of African-American boys in eighth grade were barely higher than the scores of white girls in fourth grade. In math, 46% of African-American boys demonstrated "basic" or higher grade-level skills, compared with 82% of white boys. On the National Education Longitudinal Survey, 54% of 16-year-old African-American males scored below the 20th percentile, compared with 24% of white males and 42% of Hispanic males. Having well-educated parents did not close the gap: In 2006, 43% of black high-school seniors with at least one college-educated parent failed to demonstrate even basic reading comprehension, nearly twice the percentage of whites.[7]*

A 2012 Schott Foundation for Public Education report noted that the black-white disparity in high-school graduation rates among males had narrowed by just three percentage points in the previous decade. "At this rate of progress," said the report, "... it would take another 50 years to close the graduation gap between Black males and their White male counterparts."[8]

These results are occurring despite the fact that the growth of the education workforce has far outpaced student enrollment. "Since 1970, the public school workforce has roughly doubled—to 6.4 million from 3.3 million—and two-thirds of those new hires are teachers or teachers' aides," wrote Andrew Coulson of the Cato Institute in 2012. "Over the same period, enrollment rose by a tepid 8.5%. Employment has thus grown 11 times faster than enrollment."[9] Harvard professor Paul Peterson noted that since the 1960s, per-pupil spending in the United States has more than tripled after adjusting for inflation, while the number of pupils per teacher has fallen by a third.[10]

Racial disparities in educational achievement can have serious consequences. Not surprisingly, it impacts life outcomes when the typical black student is graduating from high school (if he graduates at all) with an eighth-grade education. In general, high-school dropouts are more likely to commit crimes, abuse drugs, become teenage parents, and live in poverty. Most of the nearly half-million black students who drop out of school each year will be unemployed by their midthirties, and six in ten of the males will spend time behind bars.[11] As David Kirp noted, "among 16- to 24-year-old black men not enrolled in school, fewer than half have jobs; about a third are in prison or jail, or on probation or parole."[12] According to sociologists Christopher Jencks and Meredith Phillips, much of the black-white earning disparity can be tied to the learning gap. Young adult black men who scored above the 50th percentile on standardized tests earned 96 percent as much as their white peers in 1993, they found. And "when we compare blacks and whites with the same twelfth grade test scores, blacks are more likely than whites to complete college" and thus dramatically increase their potential lifetime earnings, among other positive outcomes.[13] As far back as the early 1980s, black couples who both were college educated earned more than their white peers.

The public continues to associate more spending with better education results, and politicians continue to tell voters what they want to hear. But for a very long time the evidence demonstrated that spending more money on schools is not key to shrinking the achievement gap. The 1966 Coleman Report, named for sociologist James Coleman, who conducted the study, surveyed 645,000 students nationwide. At the time the Lyndon Johnson administration, most education experts, and Coleman himself all expected to find a strong relationship between money spent per student and academic achievement. Instead, Coleman found that spending per pupil was about the same in both black and white schools, and that learning didn't increase based on such expenditures. "These results were acutely embarrassing to the Office of Education, the federal agency that sponsored the research," wrote Abigail Thernstrom and Stephan Thernstrom in *No Excuses: Closing the Racial Gap in Learning*.

> *. . . his findings suggested that spending more money per pupil, reducing class size, obtaining more teachers with master's degrees and the like were not likely to improve student test scores significantly in public schools as they were constituted in 1965, when the data were collected. But that was a point too subtle to convey to the press and to Congress, and the Office of Education dealt with the problem by producing a summary of the Coleman report that ignored its most important and most unsettling results.*[14]

Despite the fact that we now have nearly half a century of additional data that support these findings, politicians and the media continue to focus on spending more money, reducing class size, and hiring teachers with master's degrees—all in the name of raising achievement and closing the learning gap. Why is that? Because even though such efforts don't appear to be helping students very much, they do work to the benefit of the teachers' unions that control public education in the United States. With apologies to Baudelaire, the greatest trick the teachers' unions ever played was convincing enough people that their interests are perfectly aligned with those of schoolchildren. On the website of the United Auto Workers you will not find labor leaders posing for photos with people who have just bought Ford Fusions, because everyone knows that the UAW does not exist for the benefit of car customers. But on the website of the American Federation of Teachers cute kids are unavoidable, and even the union's mission statement claims it prioritizes the needs of the children, rather than its members. "The American Federation of Teachers," it reads, "is a union of professionals that champions fairness; democracy; economic opportunity; and high-quality public education, healthcare and public services for our students, their families and our communities."

The head of the AFT, this supposed champion for students and their families, is Randi Weingarten. "We want to improve public schools," she once told me in an interview. "Ninety percent of the kids in the United States of America go to public schools, and it's our responsibility to help them. I think every single child deserves a great education." Weingarten told the *New York Times* that "there's a much more important purpose here, which is the love of children."[15] Yet many of the policies that teachers' unions promote show utter disregard for the needs of students in general and low-income minority students in particular—not because unions don't care about kids, but because they care more about their members, notwithstanding the treacly rhetoric.

"The teachers unions have more influence over the public schools than any other group in American society," according to Terry Moe, an education scholar at Stanford. "They influence schools from the bottom up, through collective bargaining activities that shape virtually every aspect of school organization. And they influence schools from the top down, through political activities that shape government policy." Moe said the problem is not "that the unions are somehow bad or ill-intentioned. They aren't. The problem is that when they simply do what all organizations do—pursue their own interests—they are inevitably led to do things that are not in the best interests of children."[16]

The AFT and its larger sister organization, the National Education Association, have some 4.5 million dues-paying members and thousands of state and local affiliates. And it is on behalf of these members that unions fight to keep open the most violent and poorest-performing schools; block efforts to send the best teachers to the neediest students; insist that teachers be laid off based on seniority instead of performance; oppose teacher evaluation systems and merit pay structures that could ferret out bad teachers; back tenure rules that offer instructors lifetime sinecures after only a few years on the job; and make it nearly impossible to fire the system's worst actors, from teachers who are chronically absent or incompetent to those who have criminal records. None of these positions make sense if your goal is to improve public education and help children learn. But they make perfect sense if the job security of adults is your main objective.

Teachers' unions have done a masterful job of perpetuating an education establishment that prioritizes the needs of its members, even while these efforts leave black children—especially those from low-income families—demonstrably worse off. And unions have accomplished this feat primarily by making their organizations a major force in Democratic politics. Teachers' unions are not just another special interest group, like the Sierra Club or Americans for Tax Reform. They are better understood as a liberal philanthropy. They use their billions in dues money to support everything from single-payer health care to D.C. statehood to gun control. They've given money to Jesse Jackson's Rainbow PUSH Coalition, Al Sharpton's National Action Network, Bill Clinton's Global Initiative, Amnesty International, and the Gay & Lesbian Alliance Against Defamation.

"Often, the recipients of these outlays have at best a tangential education mission," wrote the *Wall Street Journal* in a 2006 editorial on the National Education Association's financial filings.

> *The Floridians For All Committee, a political action committee created by pro-labor Acorn to push for a minimum-wage hike, received $250,000 from the NEA last year. And the Fund to Protect Social Security received $400,000. In total, the NEA reports spending $25 million on "political activities and lobbying."*

In addition, reported the *Journal*, the NEA spent

> *another $65.5 million on "contributions, gifts and grants," and many of the recipients listed under this category are also overtly politicized organizations: the Congressional Black Caucus Foundation ($40,000), the Congressional Hispanic Caucus Institute ($35,000), the Democratic Leadership Council ($25,000).[17]*

But it's not just the largesse—95 percent of which goes to Democrats—that makes the AFT and NEA so essential to liberal politics. Teachers' unions are also party foot soldiers. They hand out flyers, knock on doors, work the phone banks, and ferry voters to the polls on Election Day. They typically send the most delegates to the Democratic National Convention every four years. A teachers' union endorsement, or even its decision to remain neutral in a race, can often make or break an election. It would be difficult to find another group that can match this combination of money, power, and national reach.

However the real strength of the AFT, the NEA, and their affiliates lies in their ability to obstruct policies that threaten their control of public education. When the Obama administration decided to offer grants under its Race to the Top program to states that instituted certain education reforms, it requested that the states receive buy-ins from teachers' unions before applying for the grant. Think about that. Nobody elects teachers' unions to reform education; that's why we elect politicians. Yet the "administration built the $4 billion Race to the Top contest in a way that rewarded applications crafted in consultation with labor leaders," explained the *Washington Post*.

> *The announcement that Delaware had won about $100 million highlighted that all of the state's teachers unions backed the plan for tougher teacher evaluations linked to student achievement. In second-place Tennessee, which won about $500 million, 93 percent of unions were on board.*
>
> *By contrast, applications from Florida and Louisiana were considered innovative but fell short in part because they had less union support. The District's bid, rated last among 16 finalists, was opposed by the local union.[18]*

Unions insist that the differences in outcomes between black and white students mainly reflect income disparities, which are outside the control of teachers and schools. In fact, if the education establishment is to be believed, all of the problems within public education are caused by factors outside of public education. As Weingarten put it, "Jason, don't talk to me about an achievement gap until we solve poverty in this country." Yet there is overwhelming evidence that the underprivileged black children that traditional public schools have failed so miserably are not unteachable. There have long been schools willing and able to educate the hardest cases. But many (though not all) of these schools operate outside of the traditional public-school system, so teachers' unions and their political allies work to undermine them. Again, what drives Weingarten and the politicians who carry her water is not racial animus. The simple fact is that unions have a stake in keeping kids in schools that they control, and politicians want to get elected, which is more difficult when you cross the teachers' unions.

Between 1800 and 1835, most southern states passed legislation that made it a crime to teach enslaved children how to read and write. In 1860 only about 5 percent of slaves could read. Yet "before northern benevolent societies entered the South in 1862, before President Abraham Lincoln issued the Emancipation Proclamation in 1863, and before Congress created the Bureau of Refugees, Freedom and Abandoned Lands (Freedmen's Bureau) in 1865, slaves and free persons of color had already begun to make plans for the systematic instruction of their illiterates," reported historian James Anderson. After the Civil War, wrote Harriett Beecher Stowe, "They rushed not to the grog-shop but to the schoolroom—they cried for the spelling-book as bread, and pleaded for teachers as a necessity of life." Booker T. Washington, a former slave, wrote that "few people who were not right in the midst of the scenes can form any exact idea of the intense desire which the people of my race showed for an education. . . . It was a whole race trying to go to school. Few were too young, and none too old, to make the attempt to learn."

The postwar South was "extremely hostile to the idea of universal public education. The ex-slaves broke sharply with this position," wrote Anderson. "Ex-slaves did much more than establish a tradition of education self-help that supported most of their schools. They also were the first among native southerners to wage a campaign for universal public education."[19] It did not take long for elite black schools to appear. In 1950, fewer than 10 percent of white men in the country over the age of 25 had completed four years of college. Yet between 1870 and 1955, most graduates of the District of Columbia's Dunbar High School, the first public black high school in the United States, attended college. In 1899 Dunbar's students outperformed their white peers on citywide tests. The education establishment wants to dismiss Dunbar as a fluke, but there have been too many other examples over the decades to take that rejection seriously.

Xavier University Prep, a Catholic school in New Orleans that has primarily educated blacks for nearly a century, was producing Dunbar-type results as far back as the 1950s and '60s. Amyin Parker founded the Marcus Garvey School in South Central Los Angeles in 1975, the same year that Marva Collins opened the Westside Preparatory School in Chicago. Both schools sought out poor black children and proved skeptics like Weingarten wrong. University Park Campus School, which is located in the poorest section of Worcester, Massachusetts, and accepts only neighborhood kids, opened in 1997 with thirty-five seventh graders, four of whom couldn't read. "Almost half of the entering students read at or below the third grade level and about a third were special needs students," wrote David Whitman in *Sweating the Small Stuff*, a book about successful inner-city schools. "Yet three-and-a-half years later, in tenth grade, every one of those seventh graders not only passed the state's demanding Massachusetts Comprehensive Assessment System (MCAS) English and math tests but managed to do so with high scores: more than 80 percent had proficient or advanced skills in both English and math."[20] By 2003 University Park was ranked thirty-fourth in the state (out of 332 high schools). Today some 95 percent of its students go to college, and almost all are the first in their families to do so. The people who are producing these results might take issue with Weingarten's notion that poor minorities are destined to trail whites academically "until we solve poverty in this country."

These days it is mostly charter schools that are closing the achievement gap, which is one reason why they are so popular with black people. Charter schools are tuition-free public schools run by independent organizations outside the control of the local school board. Polls have shown that charter supporters outnumber detractors two to one, and blacks who favor charters outnumber opponents by four to one. But that is less important to the education establishment than the fact that most charters aren't organized. These schools have thus earned the wrath of teachers' unions, who do everything in their power to shut them down, or at least stunt their growth. As far as the AFT and NEA are concerned, what determines whether a school reform is good or bad is not its impact on students, but its impact on adults.

Not long after my interview with Randi Weingarten I found myself listening to a speech by Geoffrey Canada, a charter-school operator in Harlem. "People are upset because I believe that these poor kids in Harlem, who have every social ill you can imagine," can still learn, said Canada. "Name one, we've got it. Gangs? Yes, we've got it. Substance abuse? Got that too. Single [parent] families? Yes, we've got all of that. Parents who don't care? Yes, we've got all of that. But my kids are going to go to college. And it doesn't matter what the issues are." Where Weingarten is making excuses, Canada is accepting responsibility. Is it any wonder that poor parents, given the opportunity, are fleeing Weingarten's schools for Canada's?

Eva Moskowitz is a former New York City councilwoman who now runs the Success Academy Charter Schools, a network of twenty-two schools in Manhattan, Brooklyn, and the Bronx serving some 6,700 children. I first met Moskowitz in 2003 when she was still a member of the city council. She headed its education committee, and decided to hold four days of hearings on what she described as the "indefensible" teachers'-union contracts that govern K–12 education in New York. My editor suggested that I interview her and sit in on the hearings. The local union, headed by Weingarten at the time, tried to stop the hearings, even though the city council had no power to change any work rules. Since Moskowitz wouldn't back down, however, the union made it clear to its members that they shouldn't cooperate. "I reached out to dozens and dozens [of teachers and principals] to talk about work rules and ask them about their ability to do their job," Moskowitz told me. People were willing to talk to her privately, but she found that requests to testify at the hearing were met with disbelief. The responses ranged from "Are you kidding?" to "I'm not that brave" to "I might be blacklisted." The upshot was that most of those who did appear at the hearings had their voices disguised and their names withheld. It was like watching a mob trial. My editorial was titled "Witness Protection for Teachers."[21]

Two years later Moskowitz would leave the city council and, in 2006, open her first school, Success Academy Harlem I, with

165 kindergarten and first-grade pupils. Within a few years the students—almost all black and Hispanic kids from low-income families—were outperforming not only their peers in traditional public schools but also white students in posh suburbs. Success Academy Harlem I, which selects students by lottery, shares a building with PS 149, one of the city's better traditional public schools. Both schools serve kids from the same racial and economic background in classes that have approximately the same number of students (the charter school's class sizes are slightly larger). But the similarities end there. In 2009, 29 percent of students at PS 149 were performing at grade level in reading and 34 percent were at grade level in math. At Harlem I—literally across the hall—the corresponding figures were 86 percent and 94 percent.[22] Ninety-seven percent of Harlem I's students passed the state exam that year, ranking it in the top one percent of all New York state public schools. Naturally these results, and her efforts to open more schools to better serve more of the city's disadvantaged kids, made Eva Moskowitz a major enemy of the New York City's education establishment.

Democracy Prep is another charter-school network that excels at teaching disadvantaged kids. It too opened its doors in Harlem in 2006 and also shared building space with a traditional public school. The results were even more shocking. "We both opened with six grades and about one hundred kids, though we had more special-ed children and English language learners," Seth Andrew, Democracy Prep's founder, once told me. "After two years in the same building with the same kids on the same floor, this school was the lowest-performing school in Harlem and we were the highest-performing school in Harlem."

Moskowitz and Andrew like to talk about test scores. So do other high-performing charter-school operators, such as David Levin and Mike Feinberg of KIPP and Geoffrey Canada of the Harlem Children's Zone. That's understandable, given their ability to improve outcomes among groups that many traditional public schools have given up on. But charter-school parents also appreciate the safer learning environment. The father of an eighth grader at Democracy Prep told me that he had pulled his son out of the district school two years earlier because of regular bullying that once left the boy hospitalized. "I just happened to get a flyer about Democracy Prep soon after that," he told me. "We entered the admissions lottery and got accepted. I didn't know anything about charters. I was just looking for an escape." He said that students at Democracy Prep are told to cross the street before walking past the district school down the block "to avoid, literally, raining textbooks—books being throw out of the school at them. That's the school my son is zoned for. If he wasn't in Democracy Prep, that's the school he'd be in—the school with the book throwers!"

Liberals who claim to care so much about underprivileged blacks not only relegate them to the worst performing schools, but also the most violent schools. The Obama administration has chastised schools for disciplining black kids at higher rates than white kids, as if racial parity in disciplinary outcomes is more important than safety. Such thinking also assumes that the suspensions reflect racial animus rather than simply which kids are acting out. But if statistical outcomes prove discrimination, what explains the fact that Asians are disciplined at lower rates than whites? Are the schools also anti-white? Liberals do no favors for blacks kids who are in school to learn by sympathizing with black kids who are in school to make trouble.

Charter-school opponents insist that the schools' superior results come from turning away kids who are more difficult to teach. "Union critics of charter schools and their supporters have repeatedly asserted that schools like Harlem Success 'skim' from the community's most intelligent students and committed families, or that they teach fewer learning-challenged or impoverished students and fewer students who are English-language learners" wrote journalist Steven Brill. "None of the actual data supports this."[23]

The best charter studies are those that use randomized experiments, which nullify self-selection bias by only comparing the kids who attend charters with those who entered the lottery but didn't win a spot. These studies, conducted by Stanford University's Caroline Hoxby, Harvard University's Thomas Kane, and the Rand Corporation, among others, have found that charter students score significantly higher on math and reading tests and are much more likely to graduate from high school and attend college.[24] A Hoxby study of New York City found that the typical charter-school student, who tends to be black and poor, is closing the achievement gap not only with his white urban peers but also with children in wealthy New York suburbs like Scarsdale. "On average," Hoxby concluded, "a student who attended a charter school for all of grades kindergarten through eight would close about 86 percent of the 'Scarsdale-Harlem achievement gap' in math and 66 percent of the achievement gap in English."[25]

When Ron Zimmer of Vanderbilt University and Cassandra Guarino of Indiana University looked at data from "an anonymous major urban school district to examine whether we see exit patterns consistent with the claim that charter schools are more likely to push out low-achieving students than traditional public schools," they found "no empirical evidence to support the notion of push-out." If anything, wrote the authors, what they found "suggests that low-performing students are more likely to transfer out of a [traditional public school] than a charter school."[26]

When Marcus Winters of the University of Colorado, Colorado Springs, looked at the special-education enrollment discrepancy between charter and traditional public schools, he found no evidence of charter-school bias against kids with disabilities. Instead, he found that children with special needs were less likely to apply to charter schools, and that traditional public schools were more likely to classify children as special-needs cases.

The gap in special education rates between charter and traditional public schools grows considerably as students progress from kindergarten through third grade. A large part (80 percent) of the growth in this gap over time is that charter schools are less likely than district schools to classify students as in need of special education services and more likely to declassify them. . . . the results do not suggest that charter schools are refusing to admit or are pushing out students with special needs. In fact, more students with previously identified disabilities enter charter schools than exit them as they progress through elementary grade levels.[27]

Other research provides clues as to why traditional schools are more likely than charters to classify a student as learning-disabled. A 2002 paper by Jay Greene and Greg Forster found that "33 states and the District of Columbia had 'bounty' funding systems, which create financial incentives to place children in special education." Greene and Forster also discovered "a statistically significant positive relationship between bounty funding systems and growth in special education enrollment."[28]

Of course, what allows charter schools to be so effective is their ability to operate outside of union rules that put the well-being of teachers ahead of students. "The Harlem Success teachers' contract drives home the idea that the school is about the children, not the grown-ups," wrote Steven Brill.

> *It is one page, allows them to be fired at will, and defines their responsibilities no more specifically than that they must help the school achieve its mission. . . . The union contract in place on the public school side of the building is 167 pages. Most of it is about job protection and what teachers can and cannot be asked to do during the 6 hours and 57.5 minutes (8:30 to about 3:25, with 50 minutes off for lunch) of their 179-day work year.*[29]

Union leaders sometimes claim that they welcome charter schools, and that may be true to the extent that they can organize them. But their actions more often than not betray an antipathy for school choice. Unions in New York first tried to prevent the state from passing a charter law. When that failed, they focused on making the law as weak as possible, primarily by capping the number of such schools that could exist. Even after charter schools in the state had demonstrated their ability to educate low-income minorities, the teachers' unions didn't give up their fight.

In 2009 New York's mayor Michael Bloomberg and schools chancellor Joel Klein announced that they were closing two persistently failing public schools in Harlem and replacing them with high-performing charters. Randi Weingarten went to war. "The schools Weingarten aimed to keep open were PS 194 and 241, notorious low performers that had both received Ds on their district report cards and, of course, were operated by members of Weingarten's union," wrote Terry Moe.

> *Parents, voting with their feet, were avoiding these two schools in droves. PS 194 had space for 628 students, but enrolled only*

288. PS 241 had space for 1,007 students, but enrolled only 310. Most parents clearly did not want their kids in those schools. The district's plan was to replace them with new charters run by Harlem Success, whose existing, nearby charters had achieved spectacular academic results. Parent desperately wanted to get their kids into these Harlem Success schools: the previous year, some 6,000 students applied for just 500 available seats.[30]

The teachers' unions filed a lawsuit to keep children in Harlem's failing schools. This scenario has played out across the country, from New York to Philadelphia to Chicago to Sacramento. After numerous interventions—more money, new curriculum, staff changes—reformers move to close persistently failing schools, and unions fight to keep them open. Again, if your goal is to do what is best for children, you steer them to schools that succeed. But if you are the teachers' unions and believe that the primary purpose of public schools is to employ your members, then you keep children trapped in the schools where your members work, and you fight to keep those schools open regardless of their quality. After all, bad teachers in bad schools still pay dues.

An even more effective reform for the urban poor that unions fight tooth and nail is the school voucher program, which allows parents to send their children to schools entirely outside the reach of the AFT and NEA. There is no disputing the fact that poor black kids who attend religious or nonsectarian institutions via vouchers perform better than their peers in traditional public schools. But that hasn't stopped liberal opposition. President Obama speaks often about the importance of staying in school, and has even urged states to raise the dropout age. At the same time he has repeatedly tried to shut down a voucher program in Washington, D.C., that serves poor minorities and produces significantly higher graduation rates than both D.C. public schools and the national average.

"President Obama proposed in his State of the Union address that teenagers be compelled to remain in school until they turn 18 or graduate," wrote Patrick Wolf of the University of Arkansas in 2012. "Who needs such Big-Brother-like compulsion? When the government provides more students with access to private schools through vouchers the kids stay in school willingly." Wolf is the U.S. Department of Education's independent evaluator of the D.C. voucher program. In 2009 the nation's fifty largest cities had an average high-school graduation rate of 53 percent.[31] But in a study published the next year, Wolf found that the D.C. voucher recipients had graduation rates of 91 percent, versus 56 percent for D.C. public schools and 70 percent for students who entered the lottery for a voucher but didn't win one. At a Senate hearing about the voucher program, officially known as the Opportunity Scholarship Program, Wolf testified that "we can be more than 99 percent confident that access to school choice through the Opportunity Scholarship Program, and not mere statistical noise, was the reason why OSP students graduated at these higher rates."[32]

Nor is Washington, D.C., the only place where access to vouchers has improved the likelihood that a minority will finish twelfth grade. A study of Milwaukee's older and larger voucher program showed a 94 percent graduation rate among students who stayed in the program throughout high school, versus a 75 percent graduation rate for their peers in the city's public schools. Not that the argument for vouchers rests entirely on high-school graduation rates. Voucher recipients have better test scores, and a 2013 study found that vouchers boosted college enrollment for blacks by 24 percent.[33] Moreover, it's less expensive to educate children using vouchers (and charter schools), which is a boon to taxpayers. And the competition from voucher programs can push traditional public schools to improve. Thus school choice indirectly benefits even those kids who don't exercise it. Education scholar Greg Forster has surveyed the large and growing body of empirical voucher studies, and summarized the key findings this way:

- *Twelve empirical studies have examined academic outcomes for school choice participants using random assignment, the "gold standard" of social science. Of these, 11 find that choice improves student outcomes—six that all students benefit and five that some benefit and some are not affected. One study finds no visible impact. No empirical study has found a negative impact.*

- *Twenty-three empirical studies (including all methods) have examined school choice's impact on academic outcomes in public schools. Of these, 22 find that choice improves public schools and one finds no visible impact. No empirical study has found that choice harms public schools.*

- *Six empirical studies have examined school choice's fiscal impact on taxpayers. All six find that school choice saves money for taxpayers. No empirical study has found a negative fiscal impact.*

- *Eight empirical studies have examined school choice and racial segregation in schools. Of these, seven find that school choice moves students from more segregated schools into less segregated schools. One finds no net effect on segregation from school choice. No empirical study has found that choice increases racial segregation.*[34]

When he ran for president in 2008 and was asked about school vouchers, Obama said that if he were presented with evidence that they improve outcomes, he would "not allow my predispositions to stand in the way of making sure that our kids can learn . . . you do what works for the kids." In fact, his administration has ignored scholars like Forster to placate teachers' unions, and has even sat on evidence of voucher success.[35] In 2013 the Justice Department sued to block a school-choice program in Louisiana that provides vouchers to poor kids to attend private institutions. Some 90 percent of the voucher recipients are black, and 86 percent of them formerly attended schools that received a D or F grade from the state. No matter. Justice argued that allowing children to leave these awful schools could make the public-school system less white in composition and hamper school desegregation efforts. Got that? To the Obama administration, the racial balance of a school is more important than whether anyone is learning.

Even if the administration's claim that school choice "frustrates and impedes the desegregation process" had merit, you might still question the logic of trying to help black people by consigning their children to the worst schools. But the claim is questionable at best, according to evidence that voucher opponents willfully ignore. *Politico* reported that

> *Louisiana hired Boston University political science Professor Christine Rossell to analyze the effect of vouchers in 34 districts in the state under desegregation orders. Rossell found that in all but four of the districts—some of which are majority white, some majority black and some more evenly split—vouchers improved or had no effect on racial imbalance. And in the districts where racial imbalance worsened, the effects were "miniscule."[36]*

A separate study out of the University of Arkansas also under-mined the notion that school choice reduces integration. "The evidence suggests that use of private school vouchers by low-income students actually has positive effects on racial integration," wrote Anna Egalite and Jonathan Mills.

> *Among the subset of students for whom data are available, we find that transfers made possible by the school-choice program overwhelmingly improve integration in the public schools that students leave (the sending schools), bringing the racial composition of the schools closer to that of the broader communities in which they are located.*[37]

Voucher opponents say they want to fix the public schools to help all kids, not just those lucky enough to get a voucher. But that's an argument for expanding, rather than limiting, school choice. And while the president and others urge poor people to sit tight until those bad schools are fixed, they themselves typically show no such patience. Obama sent his own children to private schools both before and after he became president. Bill Clinton, another anti-voucher president, also shielded his daughter from Washington's public schools. Senator Dick Durbin of Illinois, one of the fiercest opponents of the D.C. voucher program, chose private schools for his children. Even the late Ted Kennedy, considered Congress's greatest defender of public education for decades, "never found a public school good enough for his own children," wrote Sol Stern of the Manhattan Institute. Kennedy's opposition to school choice had nothing to do with whether children were better off. Rather, it was "good politics," said Stern.

> *Most of the five million government employees who work in public education are organized into highly effective unions,*

which support candidates like Kennedy and policies he favors,
such as national health insurance and affirmative action. With
support from Kennedy and others, the unions have built a Berlin
Wall that protects the public education system from competition
and prevents poor children from leaving bad schools.[38]

In education circles, public high schools that graduate 60 percent or fewer of their students on time are referred to as "dropout factories." In 2011 more than one and a half million children in the United States attended such schools, and one in four of them was black.[39] And most of the black kids who graduate have the reading and math skills of an eighth grader. Among the institutions with an acute appreciation of this sad state of affairs are the nation's historically black colleges and universities (HBCUs), which are much more likely than non-HBCUs to be faced with college freshmen who aren't college ready. Some black colleges are doing better than others, but a large majority are struggling, and on balance these schools have seen declining enrollments and low graduation rates for decades. One assessment of eighty-five of the nation's 105 black colleges found that between 2010 and 2012, nearly a third saw their enrollment decline by 10 percent or more.[40]

The reasons vary. Most of these schools were founded after the Civil War, when white institutions refused to accept blacks. Today, of course, that's no longer the case. More than 90 percent of blacks who attend college choose a non-HBCU school, and with good reason. In 2006 the six-year graduation rate at HBCUs was 37 percent, or 20 percentage points below the national average, and 8 percentage points below the average of black students at other colleges. The *Journal of Blacks in Higher Education* reported in 2012 that only four HBCUs in its survey had graduation rates above 50 percent, and at nearly half of the black colleges the graduation rate

was 33 percent or less.[41] A 2010 survey of colleges with the worst graduation rates by *Washington Monthly* magazine and Education Sector, a think tank, had black schools in the first and second place and in eight of the top twenty-four spots.

Unlike in the past, HBCU graduates today on average are worse off economically, according to a 2010 paper by Roland Fryer of Harvard and Michael Greenstone of MIT.

> *In the 1970s, HBCU matriculation was associated with higher wages and an increased probability of graduation, relative to attending a [non-HBCU school]. By the 1990s, however, there is a substantial wage penalty. Overall, there is a 20 percent decline in the relative wages of HBCU graduates over just two decades.*[42]

They concluded that black colleges

> *may have provided unique educational services for blacks in the 1970s. However by the 1990s, this advantage seems to have disappeared on many dimensions and, by some measures, HBCU attendance appears to retard black progress.*[43]

Black colleges traditionally have been heavily reliant on federal subsidies to stay afloat. Very few are capable of large capital campaigns or have substantial endowments. More than 80 percent of HBCUs get at least half of their revenue from the government. And as with K–12 education, taxpayer dollars continue to be thrown at failing schools in the name of helping blacks. In 2010 President Obama pledged to invest another $850 million in these institutions over the next decade. Some supporters of HBCUs play down their academic record and emphasize their history of educating so many consequential black professionals—including many of the civil rights leaders who helped end segregation. Others circle the wagons and are quick to dismiss any criticism of black schools as illegitimate or racially motivated. But these arguments ultimately put institutional preservation ahead of the needs of black students. The relevant issue is whether these institutions still have a role to play in black education. And the reality is that a few might, but most clearly don't—at least not as they are currently constituted.

"The glory years are long gone," wrote Bill Maxwell, who both attended and taught at an HBCU.

> Now only 1 in 5 black students earn bachelor's degrees from historically black schools, which have increasingly become dependent upon marginal students from poor families. Two-thirds of HBCU students receive federally funded Pell Grants, aimed at families earning less than $40,000 annually. More than half of the students receive those grants at every HBCU except at 13 of the best schools, such as Spelman, Howard and Morehouse.

Maxwell also described his teaching stint at Stillman, a small black college in Alabama:

> Studies show schools with a high number of Pell recipients tend to have low admission standards, and the reasons for their low graduation rates are well-documented. Most low-income students have parents who did not attend college, which often signals that their homes have few books or other reading materials. Many of the students never develop a love of learning, and they tend to perform poorly in class and on standardized tests.
>
> The statistics reflect my experience as a professor between 2004 and 2006 at Stillman, which had fewer than 1,000 stu-

dents. Most of my students would not study, regularly turn in their homework on time or read the assigned material. I walked grumbling students to the bookstore to try to force them to buy their required textbooks.

These students lacked the intellectual vigor taken for granted on traditional campuses. They did not know what or whom to respect. For many, the rappers Bow Wow and 50 Cent were at least as important to black achievement as the late Ralph Bunche, the first black to win a Nobel Peace Prize, and Zora Neale Hurston, the great novelist.

In time, I realized that my standards were too high for the quality of student I had to teach. Most simply were not prepared for college-level work, and I was not professionally trained for the intense remediation they needed and deserved. . . .

It does not help that too many black colleges have serious management issues. The media has regularly reported academic, financial or administrative problems at schools such as Morris Brown in Georgia, Lemoyne-Owen College in Memphis, Grambling State in Louisiana, Edward Waters in Jacksonville and Florida A&M in Tallahassee.

The numbers for many historically black colleges are not encouraging. Declining enrollments, loose admission standards and low graduation rates produce ever-tighter budgets, less reliable alumni networks and grimmer futures.[44]

Maxwell argued that "some schools are so academically inferior and so poorly serving their students they should be shut down," while other schools need to make some "hard choices" and rethink their mission. Cynthia Tucker, a former columnist at the *Atlanta Journal-Constitution*, agreed, writing:

There is no good reason to maintain separate-but-equal public facilities in close proximity. Today, vestiges of that outdated system remain in the form of colleges that are publicly funded and virtually all-black, frozen in place by inertia, political timidity and confusion about the mission of public institutions. Institutions supported by taxpayers should be diverse, educating men and women of all colors and creeds. There is no longer good reason for public colleges that are all-white or all-black.[45]

There are any number of reforms that might help struggling HBCUs meet today's challenges. Schools too small to continue independently could be consolidated to save money. Outside agencies, including for-profit entities, could be tapped to provide better management. Other HBCUs could be converted to community colleges that focus on remedial courses to compensate for the inferior K–12 schooling that so many black children continue to receive. These are the kinds of changes that would make HBCUs more relevant to the actual needs of black people today. And to their credit, some HBCU presidents have spoken out about the need for reform. In most cases, however, their criticism has not been well received. In 2009 word leaked that Jackson State University President Ronald Mason wanted to merge his school with two other Mississippi HBCUs. Trustees and alumni pushed back hard, and "black legislators exploded at the proposal." A short time later Mason was no longer president of Jackson State.[46]

In the past, celebrated graduates of these institutions weren't afraid to view them critically. In his biography of Thurgood Marshall, an HBCU alum, Juan Williams wrote that in the aftermath of the 1954 *Brown* decision the future Supreme Court justice spoke openly about how desegregation would impact black colleges. "What's going to happen to the 'Negro college'?" Marshall said in speeches at the time. "I'll tell you what's going to happen. It's going to cheerfully drop the word 'Negro.'" Marshall, wrote Williams, "cautioned that if these schools did not quickly measure up to the white schools, they could die off."[47]

Defenders of underperforming black colleges offer the same excuses as defenders of underperforming elementary and secondary schools. It's the students, not the schools, they insist. Yet other schools are managing to educate kids from the same backgrounds. Defending schools that are doing an awful job of teaching blacks doesn't help blacks. Black colleges certainly can be defended on school-choice grounds. If some kids perform better in an HBCU environment, or a single-sex environment, or a religious environment, there's no reason in theory why those options should not be available. But that's not an argument for sustaining black schools at all costs. Bad schools, including bad black schools, ought to reform, or close.

06

AFFIRMATIVE DISCRIMINATION

On November 3, 1983, Thomas Sowell appeared on *Firing Line*, the long-running point-counterpoint public affairs show hosted by William F. Buckley Jr. Sowell is a breathtakingly prolific intellectual based at Stanford University's Hoover Institution, and his scholarship over the past four decades is uncommonly broad, covering everything from economics to education to the history of ideas. During the 1970s and early '80s, in books like *Black Education: Myths and Tragedies*, *Race and Economics*, and *Markets and Minorities*, he established himself as something of a maverick thinker, especially when it came to questioning the basic assumptions behind popular public policies aimed at racial and ethnic minorities.

The format of *Firing Line* varied over the course of its three-decade run, but in 1983 most shows would begin with Buckley interviewing a guest on a given subject in front of a small studio audience. Then another person, typically someone with an opposing view, would question the guest. The exchanges often were sharp, but this was not combat television of the type that later would dominate cable news commentary. The tone was respectful and the pace was unhurried. Sowell's appearance coincided with the publication of his most recent book, *The Economics and Politics of Race*, a pioneering international study of discrimination. And during the first part of the program he and Buckley covered, among other things, Sowell's opposition to using racial preferences to assist poor blacks.

"The net effect of the preferential treatment, which is preferential in intention more so than in results, is that those blacks who are particularly disadvantaged have fallen further behind under these policies," Sowell declared. "Affirmative action has typically benefited people who were already well off and made them better off." As usual, Sowell cited research to support his claim.

For example, blacks who have relatively less work experience, lower levels of education, black female-headed families—all these groups have fallen further behind during a decade or more of affirmative action. Black female-headed households have had an absolute decline in real income over this span and have fallen further behind white female-headed families. At the same time, black couples who are both college educated earn higher incomes than white couples who are both college educated.

Sowell's cross-examiner that day was Robert Lekachman, a professor of economics at Lehman College of the City University of New York, who argued that racial preferences nevertheless are justified on moral and historical grounds:

> Has there not been throughout our history a whole set of formal, informal affirmative actions for white males, for Episcopalians, for graduates of Ivy League colleges . . . various clubs which are engaged in affirmative action for limited groups of their own members? In all of these clubs important business is transacted to the benefit of the members and to the exclusion of people who are not. We have affirmative action of all kinds in this country addressed to the interests of the stronger groups. Now comes a moment in our history when affirmative action, for a bit, is advanced for the benefit of groups which have been traditionally at the short end of the distribution of good things in our society, and there is considerable revulsion against it. Isn't this just a bit of historical justice that's being advanced?

Sowell was having none of it. His point, he reminded Lekachman, was that the data showed affirmative action wasn't helping the intended beneficiaries. "I simply do not see the justice in making people who are badly off worse off, in the name of advancing them."

Lekachman next challenged Sowell's claim that affirmative-action policies had been ineffective. Specifically, he took issue with Sowell contrasting black experiences in the 1960s and the 1970s, given the economic turmoil of the latter decade. "What this suggests to me is that the gains of affirmative action are extraordinarily precarious if you run an economy at low levels of activity," said Lekachman, ignoring Sowell's point that the lag in the 1970s among poor blacks had been not only absolute but also relative to that of comparable whites.

> *It's a bad comparison because the '60s were a period of expansion. With or without affirmative action, given the presence of the 1965 Civil Rights Act, given the 1954 Brown decision and the general climate of opinion. . . . Do you really think, these considerations taken into mind, that the '70s disproved the efficacy of affirmative action?*

Sowell asked why the burden of proof is on affirmative action's skeptics. "I think that when one makes a profound change in a society, arousing enormous passions across the board, that the burden of proof should be on those who think that this is beneficial," he said. "I have been listening very carefully and have yet to hear the benefit to disadvantaged blacks that has been empirically discovered after affirmative action."

Then the following exchange occurred:

LEKACHMAN: *Well, how quickly do you expect the changes? . . . The problems have been of long standing in our society. The remedy of affirmative action is a novel one. . . .*

SOWELL: *It's fascinating. . . . I see this happening on all sorts of issues, from Federal Reserve policies on across the board. You'll say, "Here's this wonderful program and it will do wonderful things, and the burden of proof is on others to show that it will not do those things." And no matter how long it's been going on, it's never long enough. If it failed, there just wasn't enough commitment, the budget wasn't big enough. It should have had a larger staff, wider powers.*

> *But there is never any sense of a burden of proof on you to say—when you've made this change that has caused such furor in this country, and has gotten people at each other's throats, including people who have been allies in the past, such as blacks and the Jews—there is never any sense of a need for you to advance the empirical evidence to support what you've been doing.*
>
> LEKACHMAN: *I'm perfectly happy to subject the affirmative-action policies to reasonable statistical evaluation, given a sufficient period.*
>
> SOWELL: *What is a sufficient [period]?. . . You said "for a bit." And now we're talking a "sufficient period." And I have difficulty with these, uh, what temporal units are you talking about? Centuries? Decades?*
>
> LEKACHMAN: *I would think of twenty to twenty-five years as a reasonable period.*

Of course, race-conscious public policies are no longer novel, and they have persisted for much longer than a quarter of a century, as have Lekachman's arguments for keeping them in place. In a 2003 landmark decision upholding the use of race in college admissions, the Supreme Court declared, like Lekachman did two decades earlier, that affirmative-action policies just needed a little more time to work their magic. "We expect that 25 years from now, the use of racial preferences will no longer be necessary," wrote Justice Sandra Day O'Connor in her majority opinion.

Several major Supreme Court rulings regarding affirmative action have involved higher education, but the concept originated in American law in response to employment discrimination. And while the beneficiaries of these policies would later include other groups—most notably, women—the impetus for the legislation was the plight of black workers.

> It shall be an unlawful employment practice for an employer . . . to fail or refuse to hire or to discharge any individual, or otherwise to discriminate against any individual with respect to his compensation, terms, conditions, or privileges of employment, because of such individual's race, color, religion, sex, or national origin,

reads the Civil Rights Act of 1964. As for enforcement, the law says that if a court

> finds that the respondent has intentionally engaged in or is intentionally engaging in an unlawful employment practice . . . the court may . . . order such affirmative action as may be appropriate, which may include, but is not limited to, reinstatement or hiring of employees, with or without back pay . . . or any other equitable relief as the court deems appropriate.

Some opponents of the bill were concerned that it would lead to quotas and timetables that required employers to hire or promote specific numbers of minorities. During the legislative debate, defenders insisted that this would not happen. Attempting to address skeptics, Senator Hubert Humphrey, the lead sponsor, noted that the measure "does not require an employer to achieve any kind of racial balance in his work force by giving any kind of preferential treatment to any individual or group." The legislation, he said, required "an intention to discriminate" before an employer would be considered in violation of the law. But as federal courts and government agencies began enforcing the new civil rights law, it didn't take long for the concept of equal opportunity to fall by the wayside, to be replaced by a concept of equal results. Policies that initially said people must be judged without regard to race and sex evolved into policies that required the consideration of those characteristics. The goalposts had moved. A year after the Civil Rights Act passed Lyndon Johnson announced that it was time for the "next and more profound stage of the battle," which he described as a battle for "not just equality as a right and a theory but equality as a fact and equality as a result."

Equal outcomes may be a noble objective, but nothing in human history suggests that they are realistic. Different groups have different backgrounds and interests and skills and sensibilities. Success and failure is not randomly distributed. By moving the public-policy emphasis away from equal opportunity, where it belonged, and toward some fanciful notion of racially proportionate results, Johnson was laying the groundwork for a civil rights industry that to this day insists that racially disparate policy outcomes are proof of discrimination, regardless of the policy's intentions.

In the American legal system, the burden of proof is on the prosecution in criminal cases and on the plaintiff in civil cases. But civil rights cases began to deviate from this tradition in 1971, when the Supreme Court handed down its decision in *Griggs v. Duke Power Co.* At issue in the case was Duke's hiring criteria for certain jobs, which included a high-school diploma and a minimal score on an IQ test. The plaintiffs argued that those requirements disqualified too many black job applicants, and amounted to employment discrimination. The court agreed, ruling that the burden of proof is on the employer when hiring criteria has a "disparate impact" on minorities. If minorities were underrepresented in a company's workforce, the employer now had to prove that discrimination was not the reason. The court said that even if the hiring requirements were "neutral on their face, and even neutral in terms of intent," they could still violate the 1964 Civil Rights Act. Differences in outcomes were now prima facie evidence of discrimination. We had moved from a focus on the rights of minority individuals to the preferential treatment of minority groups. In less than a decade, the goal had shifted from equal opportunity to statistical parity. And people who initially had been sympathetic to the black civil rights movement would feel betrayed.

"The expectation of color-blindness that was paramount in the mid-1960s has been replaced by policies setting a rigid frame of numerical requirements. They are what we have in mind today when we speak of affirmative action," wrote Nathan Glazer, the Harvard sociologist, back in 1987. "Whatever the term meant in the 1960s, since the 1970s affirmative action means quotas and goals and timetables."[1] Glazer's analysis is still true, only more so. In 2011 the Congressional Research Service, which provides policy analysis to Congress, issued a report titled "Survey of Federal Laws Containing Goals, Set-Asides, Priorities, or Other Preferences Based on Race, Gender, or Ethnicity." The document is thirty-six pages in length, and the summary describes it as "a broad, but by no means exhaustive, survey of federal statutes that specifically refer to race, gender, or ethnicity as factors to be considered in the administration of any federal program. Such measures may include, but are not limited to, goals, timetables, set-asides, quotas, priorities, and preferences, as those terms are generally (however imperfectly) understood."

Commenting on the report, Peter Kirsanow, a member of the U.S. Commission on Civil Rights, noted that in 1995 there were 172 federal statutes that granted "preferences in employment, contracting, or awarding federal benefits on the basis of membership in a preferred class." By 2011 that number had climbed to 276, said Kirsanow, writing:

> *When first employed more than 40 years ago, part of the rationale for affirmative-action programs was that they were necessary to remedy specific instances of discrimination by the federal government against certain minority groups. Yet the further we get from the era of widespread discrimination against certain minority groups, the more the federal government discriminates in favor of such groups.*[2]

No matter its original meaning or intent, affirmative action in practice today is racial discrimination. Some supporters will even admit this—and they get annoyed when fellow supporters pretend otherwise. In his book *The Audacity of Hope*, Barack Obama posits that affirmative-action programs, when properly structured, "can open up opportunities otherwise closed to qualified minorities without diminishing opportunities for white students." Randall Kennedy, a Harvard law professor and affirmative-action advocate, takes Obama to task for denying the obvious: When special efforts are made to accommodate some, you are necessarily diminishing opportunities for others.

> *Acutely sensitive to charges that he supports racial favoritism that discriminates against whites, Obama defines affirmative action in a fashion meant to drain it of controversy. . . . Racial affirmative action does distinguish between people on a racial basis. It does discriminate. It does redistribute resources. It does favor preferred racial categories of candidates, promoting some racial minorities over whites with superior records. It does*

generate stigma and resentment. These issues cannot usefully
be hidden for long behind verbal tricks.[3]

A key difference between Kennedy and Obama is that the latter
is a politician trying to obscure the true nature of affirmative-action
policies in order to maintain public support for them. A *New York
Times* poll in 2013 showed that "more than half of Americans, 53
percent, favor affirmative action programs for minorities in college
admissions and hiring," but the story added that "other surveys
that frame the question in terms of giving minorities 'preference'
find less support."[4] Thus, Obama's description of affirmative action
wins far more public support than Kennedy's. Put another way, the
more accurately you describe affirmative action, the worse it polls.

In fact, surveys going back decades—even those that avoid
words like "preferences" but frame the question fairly—have shown
that most people, including a majority of blacks, oppose racial
double standards. A 2001 *Washington Post* poll asked: "In order
to give minorities more opportunity, do you believe race or ethnicity should be a factor when deciding who is hired, promoted,
or admitted to college, or that hiring, promotions, and college
admissions should be based strictly on merit and qualifications
other than race or ethnicity?" Ninety-two percent of all respondents,
and 86 percent of blacks, answered that such decisions "should be
based strictly on merit and qualifications other than race/ethnicity."
Similarly, a 1997 *New York Times/CBS News* poll found that 69
percent of all respondents, and 63 percent of blacks, said that "race
should not be a factor" when asked how "equally qualified college
applicants" should be assessed. "Despite its wide currency," wrote
journalist Stuart Taylor, "'affirmative action' is a misleading phrase,
because most Americans interpret it as including aggressive anti-
discrimination measures, recruitment and outreach efforts, and

preferences for poor people to promote genuine equality of opportunity—policies that are in fact supported by almost all opponents of racial preferences."[5]

Foes of racial preferences have been waiting for decades for the Supreme Court to denounce this subsequent perversion of legislation, originally intended only to ensure that everyone got a fair shot. "It seems that almost every year since the middle 1970s," wrote Glazer,

> we have awaited with hope or anxiety the determination of some major case by the Supreme Court, which would either tell us that affirmative action transgressed the "equal protection of the laws" guaranteed by the Fourteenth Amendment and the apparent commitment to color-blindness of the Civil Rights Act of 1964, or, on the contrary, determine that this was a legitimate approach to overcoming the heritage of discrimination and segregation and raising the position of American blacks."[6]

The high court's 2003 decision in *Grutter v. Bollinger* upheld the use of a race-conscious admissions policy at the University of Michigan Law School. The court said that "student body diversity is a compelling state interest" that can trump the Constitution's core equal protection principles. Helpfully, it added that "all governmental use of race must have a logical end point." Unhelpfully, it failed to impose one.

Fisher v. the University of Texas at Austin, a 2013 decision, was yet another Supreme Court punt. The plaintiff, Abigail Fisher, said that the university had discriminated against her as a white woman in rejecting her application. The justices remanded the case to a lower court to review the issue under a new legal standard. As the

New York Times reported, "The 7-to-1 decision avoided giving a direct answer about the constitutionality" of the school's affirmative-action program.[7]

Justice Clarence Thomas's concurrence in *Fisher* noted that he would have not only held that the University of Texas's admissions program violated the Equal Protection Clause of the Constitution but also struck down the diversity rationale for racial preferences that the court countenanced in *Grutter*. For Thomas, state-sponsored racial discrimination is state-sponsored racial discrimination. And whether it's being advocated by 1950s-era white segregationists or twenty-first-century black liberal elites like Barack Obama and Randall Kennedy, it's unconstitutional. He wrote:

> *Unfortunately for the University, the educational benefits flowing from student body diversity—assuming they exist—hardly qualify as a compelling state interest. Indeed, the argument that educational benefits justify racial discrimination was advanced in support of racial segregation in the 1950's, but emphatically rejected by this Court. And just as the alleged educational benefits of segregation were insufficient to justify racial discrimination then . . . the alleged educational benefits of diversity cannot justify racial discrimination today.*

Thomas then went a step further, getting at the essence of what affirmative-action advocates are really positing:

> *While I find the theory advanced by the University to justify racial discrimination facially inadequate, I also believe that its use of race has little to do with the alleged educational benefits of diversity. I suspect that the University's program is instead based on the benighted notion that it is possible to tell when*

discrimination helps, rather than hurts, racial minorities. . . .
The worst forms of racial discrimination in this Nation have
always been accompanied by straight-faced representations that
discrimination helped minorities.

In an earlier opinion, *Adarand Constructors, Inc. v. Peña*, which
involved racial preferences for minority businesses, Thomas also
took on affirmative-action do-gooders.

That these programs may have been motivated, in part, by good
intentions cannot provide refuge from the principle that under
our Constitution, the government may not make distinctions
on the basis of race. As far as the Constitution is concerned, it
is irrelevant whether a government's racial classifications are
drawn by those who wish to oppress a race or by those who
have a sincere desire to help those thought to be disadvantaged.

Affirmative action is now approaching middle age. We are nearly
five decades into this exercise in social engineering. And aside from
the question of its constitutionality, there remains the matter of its
effectiveness. Do racial preferences work? What is the track record?
Have they in fact helped the intended beneficiaries? How much
credit do they deserve for the minority gains that have occurred?
Russell Nieli, a political scientist at Princeton, wrote:

While the first of the national "affirmative-action" initiatives—
Richard Nixon's Philadelphia Plan for opening up jobs in the
urban construction industry—did focus on the black inner-city
poor, it proved to be the exception as recipients of racial prefer-
ences quickly came to be the better-off, not the truly needy. . . .
Those who once occupied the preeminent place in public policy

concern—those "hobbled by chains," as Lyndon Johnson called them in his Howard University address, or the "truly disadvantaged," as William Julius Wilson later described them—fell off of the national radar screen."[8]

There is no question that black poverty fell and that the professional class swelled in the decades following the implementation of racial preferences. In 1970 blacks comprised 2.2 percent of physicians, 1.3 percent of lawyers, and 1.2 percent of engineers, according to census data. By 1990 those percentages had more than doubled. In 1967, just 5.8 percent of the black population earned more than $50,000 per year. By 1992 the proportion had climbed to 13 percent. Liberals automatically credit affirmative action, of course, but note what was already happening prior to the introduction of preferential policies in the late 1960s and early 1970s.

"By 1970 over a fifth of African-American men and over a third of black women were in middle-class occupations, *four times* as many as in 1940 in the case of men and *six times* as many in the case of women," wrote Stephan and Abigail Thernstrom, coauthors of *America in Black and White*. The authors note that between 1940 and 1970 the number of black schoolteachers nearly quadrupled, to almost a quarter of a million, while the number of social workers and registered nurses rose by even more.

Thus, there was a substantial black middle class already in existence by the end of the 1960s. In the years since, it has continued to grow, but not at a more rapid pace *than in the preceding three decades, despite a common impression to the contrary. Great occupational advances were made by African Americans before preferential policies were introduced.[9]*

The drop in black poverty that preceded the war was even more dramatic. In 1940 the black poverty rate was 87 percent. By 1960 it had fallen to 47 percent, a 40-point drop that predated not only affirmative action but the passage of landmark civil rights bills that liberals would later credit with the steep decline in black poverty. Did affirmative action play a role in reducing the percentage of poor blacks? If so, it wasn't much of one. In 1970, 33.5 percent of blacks would be living below the official poverty line. In 1990, two full decades of affirmative action later, it would be 31.9 percent. Affirmative action deserves about as much credit for the decline in black poverty as it deserves for the rise of the black middle class. In both cases, racial preferences at best continued a trend that had already begun. And in both cases the trend was considerably stronger in the decades immediately preceding affirmative-action policies than in the decades immediately following their implementation. If, as the NAACP claims every time someone spots a Confederate flag at a parade, white racism is a major barrier to group progress, how can it be that black people were rising out of poverty and into the middle class at a *faster* clip when racism in the United States was legal, socially acceptable, and rampant—none of which is the case today?

Blacks as a group, and poor blacks in particular, have performed better in the *absence* of government schemes like affirmative action. That's not an argument for returning to Jim Crow; civil rights are fundamental to a free society, and it was wrong to deny them to blacks. But it does suggest that there are limits to social engineering that arrogant politicians and public-policy makers continue to ignore.

The growth of minority professionals is encouraging, but affirmative-action policies were sold as a way to remedy the plight of the black underclass. And empirical data continue to show that isn't happening. Under affirmative action, low-income blacks have fallen farther behind. Between 1967 and 1992, incomes for the wealthiest 20 percent of blacks rose at approximately the same rate as their white counterparts. But the poorest 20 percent of blacks saw their incomes *decline*, at more than double the rate of comparable whites over the same time period. Income disparity among blacks increased at a faster rate than income disparity among whites.[10] This trend, which social scientists call "income segregation," has actually worsened in more recent years.

"Segregation by income among black families was lower than among white families in 1970, but grew four times as much between 1970 and 2007," according to a 2011 study by two Stanford University scholars. "By 2007, income segregation among black families was 60 percent greater than among white families. Although income segregation among blacks grew substantially in the 1970s and 1980s, it grew at an ever faster rate from 2000 to 2007, after declining slightly in the 1990s."[11] Again, empirical data showed that in an era of racial preferences, quotas, and set-asides ostensibly intended to help the black poor, that subset had regressed.

Of course, liberals would much rather accentuate the positive, or at least what they believe to be the beneficial results of color-conscious policies. Hence, proponents credit affirmative action with the increase in black college students and contend that ending double standards in admissions would reduce their numbers and decimate the black middle class. But is this another example of affirmative action being oversold as crucial to the success of blacks?

Affirmative action in higher education initially meant greater outreach. Until the early 1970s the goal was to seek out minorities in areas—such as the black inner city—that college recruiters at elite institutions had previously ignored. But it soon became clear that these schools couldn't possibly find a critical mass of blacks who were qualified, so they began lowering the admissions requirements for black applicants. The history of affirmative action in academia since the 1970s is a history of trying to justify holding blacks to lower standards in the name of helping them.

It's no great shock that top schools would have trouble finding blacks with the same qualifications as Asian and white applicants. Black children are more likely to attend the lowest-performing elementary schools. They leave high school with the reading and math skills of an eighth grader. And anti-intellectualism permeates black culture. "Although inequality in academic preparation is not surprising, the magnitude of the gaps is startling," wrote University of Chicago sociologists Richard Arum and Josipa Roksa, who conducted a survey for their 2011 book, *Academically Adrift*.

> *Twenty-five percent of white students reported taking no AP courses in high school, but almost twice as many (45 percent) African-American students reported no AP experience. . . . With respect to high school GPA, white students clearly fared the best: only 11 percent were in the bottom quintile of the secondary school GPA distribution. In contrast, 49 percent of African-American students and 37 percent of Hispanic students had high school GPAs in the bottom quintile. While these gaps are troubling, the gaps in SAT/ACT scores are even more so. Only 9 percent of white students scored in the bottom quintile of the SAT/ACT distribution. In contrast, more than six times as many (59 percent) African-American students scored in the bottom quintile.*[12]

Affirmative-action advocates generally downplay the racial achievement gap among entering college freshmen, but it is pronounced—particularly at more selective colleges—and has been for decades. In the early 1980s, when a perfect SAT score was 1600 and college freshmen at selective schools were averaging scores of around 1200, very few blacks came close to meeting that standard. In 1981 seventy thousand blacks took the SAT, and fewer than one thousand of them (1.2 percent) scored as high as 600 (out of 800) on the verbal portion. By comparison, nearly fifty-eight thousand white test takers, or 8 percent of the total, had verbal scores that high, which put the ratio of whites to blacks at 61 to 1. And the racial differences in math were even larger.[13]

Between 1978 and 1988 the scores of black freshmen at the University of California, Berkeley, trailed white test scores by between 250 and 332 points on average. The gap between whites and Asians over the same period averaged between 54 and 91 points, with whites leading in some years and Asians leading in others.[14] Berkeley is a selective school, and in the late 1980s and early 1990s a typical freshman there had an SAT score in excess of 1200 points. Yet between 1990 and 1994 the nationwide SAT score among whites and Asians averaged around 945. Among blacks, it was about 740. That gives you some indication of how difficult it would have been for Berkeley to find black students who met its normal standards. And while Berkeley is selective, it's not Harvard or Yale or Stanford or MIT, where average SAT scores in the 1990s were closer to 1300.

By 1995 blacks had made gains, but the racial gap remained quite large. The percentage of blacks scoring above 600 on the verbal section of the SAT that year rose to 1.7 percent, versus 9.6 percent among whites. So for every black student who scored that high, there were thirty-seven whites who did the same. The SAT added a writing portion in 2006, and blacks have lagged badly in that category as well. The 2012 black test scores trailed white test scores by 99 points in reading, 108 points in math, and 98 points in writing—and were well below the national average in all three categories.

These gaps and ratios are relevant because defenders of racial preferences like to pretend that affirmative action is an innocuous policy that simply gives a slight edge to otherwise qualified black applicants. Or they insist that race is just one factor among many that colleges consider. But if race were simply being used as a tiebreaker by admissions officers, there is no way the nation's top schools could boast as many black students as they do. In 2011 the percentage of black freshmen at the nation's eight Ivy League colleges ranged from 7.9 percent at Cornell to 12.5 percent at Columbia. Other very selective schools, including Duke, Vanderbilt, Stanford, and MIT, also reported freshman classes in 2011 that were more than 8 percent black.[15]

As the *Journal of Blacks in Higher Education* noted in 2005, these outcomes are all but impossible if black applicants are held to the same standards as whites and Asians.

> *In a race-neutral competition for the approximately 50,000 places for first-year students at the nation's 25 top-ranked universities, high-scoring blacks would be buried by a huge mountain of high-scoring non-black students. Today, under prevailing affirmative action admissions policies, there are about 3,000 black first-year students matriculating at these 25 high-ranking universities, about 6 percent of all first-year students at these institutions. But if these schools operated under a strict race-neutral admissions policy where SAT scores were the most important qualifying yardstick, these universities could fill their freshman classes almost exclusively with students who score at the very top of the SAT scoring scale. As shown previously,*

black students make up at best between 1 and 2 percent of these high-scoring groups.

Obviously there is nothing wrong with top schools wanting to attract students from different backgrounds, but how they pursue that goal is important. "If there was a way to enroll more under-represented minorities without considering race, we'd do it," said the dean of the University of Michigan's law school. "It's not that we like being race-conscious."[16] But that begs the question of whose interests are being served. Black law-school graduates fail the bar exam at four times the white rate. Michigan's law school likes to tout its diversity, but is it doing black students any favors by admitting them with lower standards and setting them up to fail? The left believes that the large black-white gap in academic credentials among college freshmen doesn't matter, or that racial and ethnic diversity is a bigger concern. Schools go out of their way to hide information on admissions and student outcomes. But what if these efforts to color-code campuses at any cost are not so benign? Putting aside the constitutionality of race-based college admissions, a separate question is whether black students are helped or harmed when they are admitted to a school with lower qualifications than those required of other students at the same institution. Fortunately, we don't have to speculate about the answer, because some states have banned the use of race in college admissions, and enough time has now elapsed to evaluate the results.

In 2013 the *New York Times* ran a front-page story on the University of California system's efforts to maintain a racially and ethnically diverse student body without using group quotas, which had been banned in the state seventeen years earlier. "California was one of the first states to abolish affirmative action, after voters approved Proposition 209 in 1996," wrote the *Times*. "Across the University of California system, Latinos fell to 12 percent of newly enrolled state residents in the mid-1990s from more than 15 percent, and blacks declined to 3 percent from 4 percent. At the most competitive campuses, at Berkeley and Los Angeles, the decline was much steeper." The article went on to acknowledge that "eventually, the numbers rebounded" and that "a similar pattern of decline and recovery followed at other state universities that eliminated race as a factor in admissions."[17] And given all of the dire predictions made at the time, it's nice to see that the worse-case scenarios didn't come to pass. But the too-seldom-told story of affirmative action in the University of California system is the black *gains* that have occurred since it was abolished.

In their book, *Mismatch*, authors Richard Sander and Stuart Taylor Jr. tell this good-news story by comparing the pre- and post-Proposition 209 eras. Here is a sample of their findings:

- *The number of blacks entering UC as freshmen in 2000 through 2003 is, on average, only 2 percent below pre-209 levels, and black enrollment jumps when we take into account transfers and lower attrition.*
- *The number of Hispanic freshmen is up by 22 percent over the same period, and again more when we include transfers.*
- *The number of blacks receiving bachelor degrees from UC schools rose from an average of 812 in 1998–2001 (the final cohorts entirely comprised of pre-209 entrants) to an average of 904 in 2004–2007 (the first cohorts entirely comprised of post-209 entrants). For UC Hispanics, the numbers rose from 3,317 to 4,428.*

- *The number of UC black and Hispanic freshmen who went on to graduate in four years rose 55 percent from 1995–1997 to 2001–2003.*
- *The number of UC black and Hispanic freshmen who went on to graduate in four years with STEM [science, technology, engineering, and math] degrees rose 51 percent from 1995–1997 to 2001–2003.*
- *The number of UC black and Hispanic freshmen who went on to graduate in four years with GPAs of 3.5 or higher rose by 63 percent from 1995–1997 to 2001–2003.*
- *Doctorates and STEM graduate degrees earned by blacks and Hispanics combined rose by one-quarter from cohorts starting in 1995–1997 to cohorts starting in 1998–2000.*[18]

Prior to the passage of Proposition 209, blacks and Hispanics in California were steered into schools where they were under-prepared relative to the other students. They were being "mismatched" to satisfy the cosmetic concerns of administrators, to embellish photographs in school brochures. "Diversity" was deemed more important than learning. Proponents of racial preferences weren't overly concerned with whether these minorities actually graduated, and many of them didn't (or only did so by switching to a less demanding major). After race preferences were banned, blacks and Hispanics were more likely to attend a school where they could handle the work, and as a result many more of them have flourished academically.

Yes, fewer minorities attended Berkeley and UCLA in the wake of the new policy, and instead matriculated at less selective places like UC Santa Cruz, but more minorities overall not only graduated, but obtained degrees in engineering and science. What's more important? Once again empirical data show blacks doing better in the absence of a government policy originally put in place to help them. Once again the political left, which has a vested interest in convincing black people that group success is highly dependent on policies like affirmative action, has ignored or downplayed results at odds with its agenda.

Members of the U.S. Commission on Civil Rights have noted the "extensive empirical research indicating that students who attend schools where their entering academic credentials put them in the bottom of the class are less likely to follow through with an ambition to major in science or engineering than similarly-credentialed students who attend schools where their credentials put them in the middle or top of the class. Affirmative action thus works to the detriment of its supposed beneficiaries." Furthermore, "students, regardless of race, are less likely to graduate from law school and pass the bar if they are the beneficiaries of preferential treatment in admissions than if they attend a law school at which their entering academic credentials are like the average student's."[19] Researchers at Duke University, where blacks are admitted with SAT scores much lower than those of whites and Asians, found that more than 76 percent of black male freshmen intended to major in the hard sciences, which made them more likely than their white peers to pick those majors. The *Weekly Standard* reported:

> But more than half of those would-be black science majors switched track in the course of their studies, while less than 8 percent of white males did, so that by senior year, only 35 percent of black males graduated with a science or economics degree, while more than 63 percent of white males did. Had those minority students who gave up their science aspirations taken Introductory Chemistry among students with similar levels of academic preparation, they would more likely have continued

with their original course of study, as the unmatched record of
[generally less selective] historically black colleges in graduating
science majors suggests.[20]

Most of these students are capable of succeeding in majors of
their choosing at good schools that are less selective. But affirmative-
action policies work against them. As Sander and Taylor noted,

> *It is not lack of talent or innate ability that drives these students*
> *to drop out of school, flee rigorous courses, or abandon aspira-*
> *tions to be scientists or scholars; it is, rather, an unintended*
> *side effect of large racial preferences, which systematically put*
> *minority students in academic environments where they feel*
> *overwhelmed . . .*
>
> *The student who would flourish at, say, Wake Forest or the*
> *University of Richmond, instead finds herself at Duke, where*
> *professors are not teaching at a pace designed for her—they are*
> *teaching to the "middle" of the class, introducing terms and*
> *concepts at a speed that is challenging even to the best-prepared*
> *student.*[21]

In addition to producing fewer black professionals than we
would have under race-neutral policies, affirmative action comes with
a stigma and reinforces ugly stereotypes of black inferiority. "When
few Jews could get into Ivy League schools, and Jewish students
had to be superqualified to gain admission, a Jewish stereotype was
created: Jews are smart," wrote Stephan and Abigail Thernstrom.
"Admitting black students by *lower* standards has precisely the opposite effect: It reinforces the pernicious notion that blacks are not
academically talented."[22] Some liberals claim that these concerns
are trivial, or outweighed by social-justice aims of affirmative-action

policies. "I do not feel belittled by this," wrote Randall Kennedy, explaining how racial preferences were responsible for his admission to Yale Law School and any number of professional organizations:

Nor am I wracked by angst or guilt or self-doubt. I applaud the effort to rectify wrongs and extend and deepen desegregation in every aspect of American life.

There will be those, I suspect, who will put a mental asterisk next to my name upon learning that my race (almost certainly) counted as a plus in selecting me for induction into these organizations. If they do, then they should also insist upon putting a mental asterisk next to the name of any white person who prevailed in any competition from which minorities were excluded.[23]

Or, as Thurgood Marshall once put it to fellow Supreme Court Justice William Douglas, "You guys have been practicing discrimination for years. Now it's our turn."[24]

But others are less glib. In *Reflections of an Affirmative Action Baby*, Stephen Carter relates the experience of initially being denied admission to Harvard Law School in the late 1970s, but then being accepted after the school realized he was black. Several days after receiving his rejection letter, "two different Harvard officials and a professor" phoned him to apologize. "We assumed from your record that you were white," one of them said.

"Naturally, I was insulted," wrote Carter, adding,

Stephen Carter, the white male, was not good enough for the Harvard Law School; Stephen Carter, the black male, not only was good enough but rated agonized telephone calls urging him to attend. And Stephen Carter, color unknown, must have been white: How else could he have achieved what he did in

165

*college? Except that my college achievements were obviously not
sufficiently spectacular to merit acceptance had I been white.*[25]

Carter would go on to attend Yale Law School instead, where
future Supreme Court Justice Clarence Thomas had recently obtained
his law degree after doing undergraduate work at the College of the
Holy Cross. In Thomas's memoir he wrote about the evolution of
affirmative-action policies in the 1970s and how they impacted black
outcomes. "My class at Holy Cross had contained only six blacks,
but none of us failed to graduate on time, and most did very well
academically," he noted.

*By the time I joined the board of trustees in 1978, though, very
few of the black students who came to Holy Cross graduated
in the top half of their classes, and the attrition rate for blacks
in predominantly white colleges and universities throughout
America was disturbingly high. Almost half failed to graduate
on time, if at all.*[26]

Thomas wrote that when he left law school and tried to find a
job, employers assumed that he had benefited from preferential
treatment and couldn't do the work, notwithstanding his good
grades and fancy degree. "Now I knew what a law degree from
Yale was worth when it bore the taint of racial preferences. I was
humiliated."[27]

Of course, blacks aren't the only ones who struggle with the
ambiguous benefits of group preferences. In 2012, when Harvard
Law professor Elizabeth Warren was accused of claiming Native
American ancestry to take advantage of hiring policies that favor
minorities, she became indignant. Warren, a liberal Democrat who
was running for the U.S. Senate when news broke that she self-

identified as Native American in legal directories and that Harvard had showcased her as a Native American professor in the 1990s, responded to the revelations by telling everyone who would listen that she was hired based on merit alone. "I got what I got because of the work I've done," she said.[28] Supporters of affirmative action say there's no shame in being hired to meet a racial or ethnic quota instead of for your job skills alone, or in being admitted to a college with SAT scores well below those of your white and Asian peers. But the reality is that nobody who has any pride wants to be that "diversity" hire in the office or that token minority on campus, especially if it allows others to dismiss your accomplishments as having resulted from a tilted playing field.

Finally, affirmative-action debates, particularly in higher education, tend to focus on how whites, blacks, and Hispanics are impacted. But increasingly the group that has the most to lose in our racial spoils system is Asians. In 2012, when the Supreme Court agreed to hear *Fisher v. University of Texas*, four Asian American organizations filed a brief urging the court to ban race-conscious admissions.[29] The brief argued that racial preferences intended to help black applicants are detrimental not only to whites but also to Asians. It said that admission to the nation's top schools is a zero-sum proposition.

As aspiring applicants capable of graduating from these institutions outnumber available seats, the utilization of race as a "plus factor" for some inexorably applies race as a "minus factor" against those on the other side of the equation. Particularly hard-hit are Asian-American students, who demonstrate academic excellence at disproportionately high rates but often find the value of their work discounted on account of either their race, or nebulous criteria alluding to it.[30]

167

In the past Asian advocacy groups typically have stood with their black and Latino counterparts to support racial preferences in college admissions, even though Asians have the most to gain from the elimination of these policies. More selective institutions especially are worried about Asian students being overrepresented on campus, so they find ways to cap their numbers. In 1995, for example, Asian freshman enrollment at Berkeley was about 37 percent. The next year California banned racial preferences, and by 2005 Asians comprised nearly 47 percent of Berkeley's freshman class. Going forward, defenders of affirmative action will have to explain why blacks deserve preference over Asians to address the past behavior of whites.

CONCLUSION

The civil rights struggles of the mid-twentieth century were liberalism at its best. The efforts culminated in the passage of the Civil Rights Act of 1964 and the Voting Rights Act of 1965, which outlawed racial discrimination in employment and education and ensured the ability of blacks to register and vote. This book's intention is not to downplay the accomplishments of Thurgood Marshall, Rosa Parks, Martin Luther King Jr., the Freedom Riders, the NAACP, and others who helped to destroy significant barriers to black progress and make America more just. Rather, my goal is to assess some of the social policy and thinking that arose from the ruins of Jim Crow. Good intentions aside, which efforts have facilitated black advancement, and which efforts have impeded it?

In 1988, nearly a quarter of a century after the Great Society initiatives were launched, Nathan Glazer published *The Limits of Social Policy*, a critical assessment of two decades' worth of programs that were premised on the liberal belief that government action is the best way to improve the lot of people and their communities. "Against the view that to every problem there is a solution, I came to believe that we can have only partial and less than wholly satisfying answers to the social problems in question," Glazer wrote. "Whereas the prevailing wisdom was that social policies would make steady progress in nibbling away at the agenda of problems set by the forces of industrialization and urbanization, I came to believe that although social policy had ameliorated some of the problems we had inherited, it had also given rise to other problems no less grave in their effect on human happiness."

Unlike Glazer, many liberals today, still riding high on those good intentions, don't seem particularly interested in reconsidering what has been tried, even though fifty years into the war on poverty the picture isn't pretty. While gains have been made, significant racial disparities persist in some areas and black retrogression has occurred in others. The black-white poverty gap has widened over the last decade and the poverty rate among blacks is no longer declining. The black-white disparity in incarceration rates today is larger than it was in 1960. And the black unemployment rate has, on average, been twice as high as the white rate for five decades. In fact, black America has long been stuck in a severe recession. Between 1963 and 2012 annual black unemployment averaged 11.6 percent, while the average annual national unemployment rate during recessions over the same period was only 6.7 percent.

Confronted with these statistics, liberals continue to push for the same "solutions" that clearly haven't worked before. In 2014 President Obama announced yet another federal initiative aimed at helping blacks. He called for more preschool education, even though studies—like the one on Head Start released by his administration in 2012—have found "no significant impacts" in education from such programs. Obama said that he wants to increase reading proficiency and graduation rates for minority students, yet he opposes school voucher programs that are doing both. And he called for more of the same job-training programs that liberal politicians have been pushing for decades despite scant evidence of their effectiveness.

"The gains from participation are, at best, very modest, even three to four years after entry," reads a report prepared for the Labor Department on the benefits of the federal government's biggest job-training program. "Overall, it appears possible that ultimate gains from participation are small or nonexistent." That report was released by the Obama administration in 2009.

In his history of American liberalism, *The Revolt Against the Masses*, Fred Siegel wrote of a "liberal flight from evidence and empiricism" on racial matters beginning in the 1960s. The political left, wracked by guilt over America's diabolical treatment of blacks, decided to hold them to different standards of behavior. "African Americans were invited to enter into the larger society on their own terms. The schools, which had once helped set white-skinned peasants on the path to success, ceased incorporating dark-skinned peasants from the backward South into mainstream culture," wrote Siegel. "Discipline as a prerequisite for adult success was displaced by the authentic self-expression of the ill-educated. The newcomers, it was said, were not culturally deprived; they were 'differently abled,' more spontaneous and expressive." Liberals naively sought to improve conditions for blacks without passing judgment on antisocial black culture. "Like devout Christians getting right with Jesus, liberals struggled to get right with racism," wrote Siegel. "They wanted to help blacks in the worst way, and that's just what they did."

After George Zimmerman was acquitted in the shooting death of Trayvon Martin, President Obama explained the black response to the verdict in this way: "They understand that some of the violence that takes place in poor black neighborhoods around the country is born out of a very violent past in this country, and that the poverty and dysfunction that we see in those communities can be traced to a very difficult history." Obama was doing exactly what liberals have been conditioning blacks to do since the 1960s, which is to blame black pathology on the legacy of slavery and Jim Crow laws. And the president is conditioning the next generation of blacks to do the same.

But this is a dodge. Those legacies are not holding down blacks half as much as the legacy of efforts to help them "overcome." The left's sentimental support has turned underprivileged blacks into playthings for liberal intellectuals and politicians who care more about clearing their conscience or winning votes than advocating behaviors and attitudes that have allowed other groups to get ahead. Meanwhile, the civil rights movement of King has become an industry that does little more than monetize white guilt. King and his contemporaries demanded black self-improvement despite the abundant and overt racism of his day. King's successors, living in an era when public policy bends over backward to accommodate blacks, nevertheless insist that blacks cannot be held responsible for their plight so long as someone somewhere in white America is still using the n-word.

Liberalism has also succeeded, tragically, in convincing blacks to see themselves first and foremost as victims. Today there is no greater impediment to black advancement than the self-pitying mindset that permeates black culture. White liberals think they are helping blacks by romanticizing miscreants. And black liberals are all too happy to hustle guilty whites. The result, manifest in everything from black studies programs to black media to black politics, is an obsession with racial slights real or imagined.

Supreme Court Justice Clarence Thomas touched on this phenomenon when he told an audience that 2014 America seems more color conscious than when he was growing up in the segregated South. "My sadness is that we are probably today more race- and difference-conscious than I was in the 1960s when I went to school. To my knowledge, I was the first black kid in Savannah, Georgia, to go to a white school. Rarely did the issue of race come up," Thomas said. "Now, name a day it doesn't come up. Differences in race, differences in sex, somebody doesn't look at you right, somebody says something. Everybody is sensitive. If I had been as sensitive as that in the 1960s, I'd still be in Savannah. Every person in this room has endured a slight. Every person. Somebody has said something that has hurt their feelings or did something to them—left them out."

Liberals immediately went about setting Thomas straight. Charles Blow, a black *New York Times* columnist, informed the associate justice that "the racial reality of blacks in the South in the 1960s was that race- and difference-consciousness was virtually inescapable, and often stifling." Never mind that Blow was born in 1970, while Thomas was born in 1948. "It's unclear to me," continued Blow, "whether Thomas is being amnesiac in his recollections or if he was contemporaneously oblivious. Either way, being unable to acknowledge and articulate the basic fact that race was—and remains—a concern for others is disturbing."

Much more disturbing is that half a century after the civil rights battles were fought and won, liberalism remains much more interested in making excuses for blacks than in reevaluating efforts to help them.

ACKNOWLEDGMENTS

A special debt of gratitude goes to the Arthur N. Rupe Foundation and Searle Freedom Trust. I also want to thank David DesRosiers, Roger Kimball, Sam Schneider, Kacey Chuilli, and Carol Mann. I've had the good fortune to work at the *Wall Street Journal* for the past twenty years, where I developed the ideas explored in this book. I thank all of my colleagues on the editorial page for their support and encouragement. Finally, my wife, Naomi, made it possible for me to write at home during evenings and on weekends with three small children around. She then read and helped edit the manuscript. I thank her for her insights, her patience, and her indulgence.

ENDNOTES

CHAPTER ONE

1. Robert Pear, "Median Income Rises, but Is Still 6% Below Level at Start of Recession in '07," *New York* Times, August 21, 2013.

2. Andrew Kirell, "Tavis Smiley: Black People Are Not Better Off Under Obama," *Mediaite*, October 12, 2013, http://www.mediaite.com/tv/tavis-smiley-black-people-are-not-better-off-under-obama-president-ought-to-be-held-responsible/.

3. Carol M. Swain, *The New White Nationalism in America: Its Challenge to Integration* (Cambridge University Press, 2002), 403.

4. Fredrick C. Harris, "The Price of a Black President," *New York Times*, October 27, 2012.

5. See, for example, the *Washington Post* poll results published in August 2012 showing that 74 percent of all respondents, and 65 percent of blacks, expressed support for voter ID laws, http://www.washingtonpost.com/page/2010-2019/Washington Post/2012/08/12/National-Politics/Polling/question_6226 .xml?uuid=Nd4PSOTWEeGXOe75nF-yhQ.

6. Department of Justice, http://www.justice.gov/iso/opa/ag /speeches/2011/ag-speech-111213.html.

7. NPR, "Voting Rights: What's a Reasonable Requirement?" December 18, 2011, http://www.npr.org/2011/12/18/143916145 /voting-rights-whats-a-reasonable-requirement.

8. David B. Muhlhausen, "Photo ID Laws Do Not Reduce Turnout," Heritage Foundation, May 5, 2009, http://www.heritage.org /research/testimony/photo-id-laws-do-not-reduce-voter-turnout.

9. Artur Davis, "Alabama Voices: Should Have Supported Voter ID Law," *Montgomery Advertiser*, October 17, 2011.

10. Bureau of the Census, "Blacks Voted at a Higher Rate Than Whites in 2012 Election—A First, Census Bureau Reports," press release, May 8, 2013, http://www.census.gov/newsroom/releases /archives/voting/cb13-84.html.

11. Janell Ross, "Grim Economic Picture Hasn't Shaken African American Support for Obama," *Huffington Post*, August 31, 2011.

12. Clarence Thomas, *My Grandfather's Son: A Memoir* (Harper, 2007), 178–79.

13. Norman Podhoretz, ed., *The Commentary Reader: Two Decades of Articles and Stories* (Atheneum, 1966), 412.

14. Joseph M. Bessette, ed., *Toward a More Perfect Union: Writings of Herbert J. Storing* (AEI Press, 1995), 257.

15. Michael C. Dawson, *Not in Our Lifetimes: The Future of Black Politics* (University of Chicago Press, 2011), viii, ix.

16. Robert J. Norrell, *Up From History: The Life of Booker T. Washington* (Belknap Press, 2009), 13.

17. Ibid., 15, 16.

18. David Remnick, "Going the Distance: On and Off the Road With Barack Obama," *New Yorker*, January 27, 2014, http://www.newyorker.com/reporting/2014/01/27/140127fa_fact_remnick?currentPage=all

19. Ibid., 16.

20. Michael A. Fletcher, "Fifty Years After March on Washington, Economic Gap Between Blacks, Whites Persists," *Washington Post*, August 27, 2013.

21. Thomas Sowell, *Civil Rights: Rhetoric or Reality?* (Quill, 1984), 32.

22. Michael Barone, *The New Americans: How the Melting Pot Can Work Again* (Regnery, 2001), 17.

23. Ibid., 20.

24. Ibid., 21, 22.

25. Gary Orfield and Carole Ashkinaze, *The Closing Door: Conservative Policy and Black Opportunity* (University of Chicago Press, 1991), 4–7.

26. J. Harvie Wilkinson III, *From Brown to Bakke: The Supreme Court and School Integration: 1954–1978* (Oxford University Press, 1979), 236.

27. Abigail Thernstrom, *Voting Rights—and Wrongs: The Elusive Quest for Racially Fair Elections* (AEI Press, 2009), 6.

28. Ibid., 9.

29. Roger Clegg and Joshua P. Thompson, "Two Points on *Shelby County v. Holder*," *National Review Online*, February 25, 2013, http://www.nationalreview.com/bench-memos/341443/two-points-ishelby-county-v-holderi-roger-clegg.

30. Thernstrom, *Voting Rights—and Wrongs*, 20.

31. Henry Louis Gates Jr. and Cornel West, *The Future of the Race* (Vintage Books, 1997), 33.

32. Ibid., 36–37.

33. Douglas A. Blackmon, "Who Powered the Passage of the Charter School Amendment in Georgia?" (blog), November 8, 2012, http://www.slaverybyanothername.com/blog/who-powered -the-passage-of-the-charter-school-amendment-in-georgia-african -americans-who-have-been-chronically-denied-good-public-schools/.

34. Tracey McManus, "Georgia Legislative Caucus to Join Law-suit Against Gov. Nathan Deal Over Charter School Amendment," *Augusta Chronicle*, November 11, 2012.

35. David Remnick, *The Bridge: The Life and Rise of Barack Obama* (Knopf, 2010), 24.

CHAPTER TWO

1. Margaret Mead, *Male and Female: A Study of the Sexes in a Changing World* (Dell, 1968), 195–98.

2. Luke Rosiak, "Fathers Disappear From Households Across America," *Washington Times*, December 25, 2012.

3. Kareem Abdul-Jabbar and Peter Knobler, *Giant Steps: The Autobiography of Kareem Abdul-Jabbar* (Bantam Books, 1983), 16.

4. John U. Ogbu, *Black American Students in an Affluent Suburb: A Study of Academic Disengagement* (Lawrence Erlbaum Associates, 2003), 35.

5. Ibid., 23.

6. Ibid., 24, 25.

7. Felicia R. Lee, "Why Are Black Students Lagging?" *New York Times*, November 30, 2002.

8. Ogbu, *Black American Students*, 222.

9. Ibid., 255.

10. Geneva Gay, *Culturally Responsive Teaching: Theory, Research and Practice* (Teachers College Press, 2010), 23–24, 27.

11. Brian M. Rosenthal, "'Alarming' New Test-Score Gap Discovered in Seattle Schools," *Seattle Times*, December 19, 2011.

12. Yasmeen Khan, "Most Eighth Graders Matched to a High School of Their Choice," WNYC, March 15, 2013, http://www.wnyc.org/story/301978-high-school-admissions/.

13. Beth Fertig, "Around Sunset Park, Tutoring Is Key to Top High Schools," WNYC, March 12, 2013, http://www.wnyc.org/story/301916-around-sunset-park-tutoring-is-key-to-top-high-schools/.

14. Shelby Steele, *The Content of Our Character: A New Vision of Race in America* (HarperPerennial, 1990), 95, 96.

15. Robert Christgau and Greg Tate, "Chuck D All Over the Map," *Village Voice*, October 22, 1991.

16. Cornel West, *The Cornel West Reader* (Basic Civitas Books, 1999), 482.

17. Michael Eric Dyson, *The Michael Eric Dyson Reader* (Basic Civitas Books, 2004), 408, 416.

18. James P. Comer and Alvin F. Poussaint, *Raising Black Children* (Plume, 1992), 252, 357.

19. Niko Koppel, "Are Your Jeans Sagging? Go Directly to Jail," *New York Times*, August 30, 2007.

20. Juan Williams, *Enough: The Phony Leaders, Dead-End Movements, and Culture of Failure That Are Undermining Black America—and What We Can Do About It* (Three Rivers Press, 2006).

21. Michael Eric Dyson, *Is Bill Cosby Right? Or Has the Black Middle Class Lost Its Mind?* (Basic Civitas Books, 2005).

22. Ta-Nehisi Coates, "This Is How We Lost to the White Man," in *Best African American Essays 2010*, eds. Gerald Early and Randall Kennedy (One World/Ballantine, 2009), 161, 168.

23. Nathan Glazer, *The Limits of Social Policy* (Harvard University Press, 1988), 13.

24. "Idea Broker in the Race Crisis," *Life*, November 3, 1967. Cited in Charles Murray, *Losing Ground: American Social Policy, 1950–1980 (Tenth-Anniversary Edition)* (Basic Books, 1994), 29.

25. "Black America: Waking Life," *The Economist*, August 24, 2013.

26. Thomas Sowell, *Black Rednecks and White Liberals* (Encounter, 2005), 6.

CHAPTER THREE

1. Cited in Dinesh D'Souza, *The End of Racism* (Free Press, 1995), 267.

2. Linn Washington, *Black Judges on Justice: Perspectives from the Bench* (New Press, 1995), 71.

3. "Book Discussion on *Black Judges on Justice*," C-SPAN video, 59:02, April 20, 1995, http://www.c-spanvideo.org/videoLibrary /transcript/transcript.php?programid=142160.

4. Michelle Alexander, *The New Jim Crow: Mass Incarceration in the Age of Colorblindness* (New Press, 2010), 11.

5. Ibid., 16.

6. Ibid., 4.

7. Ibid., 148.

8. Ibid., 138.

9. Ibid., 192.

10. Rick Perlstein, *Nixonland: The Rise of a President and the Fracturing of America* (Scribner, 2008), 343.

11. Thomas Sowell, *The Vision of the Anointed: Self-Congratulation as a Basis for Social Policy* (Basic Books, 1995), 28.

12. William J. Stuntz, *The Collapse of American Criminal Justice* (Belknap Press, 2011), 37.

13. Lucas A. Powe Jr., *The Warren Court and American Politics* (Belknap Press, 2000), 408.

14. James Q. Wilson and Richard J. Herrnstein, *Crime and Human Nature: The Definitive Study of the Causes of Crime* (Free Press, 1985), 29, 461.

15. Stuntz, *Criminal Justice*, 21.

16. Heather Mac Donald, "Distorting the Truth About Crime and Race," *City Journal*, May 14, 2010, http://www.city-journal.org/2010/eon0514hm.html.

17. Heather Mac Donald, "Is the Criminal-Justice System Racist?", *City Journal* 18 (Spring 2008), http://www.city-journal.org/2008/18_2_criminal_justice_system.html.

18. Ibid.

19. Randall Kennedy, *Race, Crime, and the Law* (Pantheon, 1997), 371–72.

20. Alexander, *Jim Crow*, 214.

21. Mac Donald, "Is the Criminal-Justice System Racist?", http://www.city-journal.org/2008/18_2_criminal_justice_system.html.

22. Wilson and Herrnstein, *Crime and Human Nature*, 473.

23. John Lott, "Stand Your Ground Makes Sense," *New York Daily News*, April 25, 2012.

24. Emily Alpert, "Gun Crime Has Plunged, but Americans Think It's Up, Says Study," *Los Angeles Times*, May 7, 2013.

25. John R. Lott Jr., "Reforms That Ignore the Black Victims of Crime," *Cato Unbound*, March 13, 2009, http://www.cato-unbound.org/2009/03/13/john-r-lott-jr/reforms-ignore-black-victims-crime.

26. Franklin E. Zimring, *The Great American Crime Decline* (Oxford University Press, 2007), v.

27. Ibid., 5.

28. Ibid., vi.

29. Ibid., vi.

30. James Q. Wilson, "Hard Times, Fewer Crimes," *Wall Street Journal*, May 28, 2011.

31. Heather Mac Donald, "Courts v. Cops," *City Journal* 23 (Winter 2013), http://www.city-journal.org/2013/23_1_war-on-crime.html.

32. Layne Weiss, "NAACP Introduces 'Trayvon's Law,'" *Digital Journal*, August 2, 2013, http://www.digitaljournal.com/article /355702.

33. Shelby Steele, "The Decline of the Civil-Rights Establishment," *Wall Street Journal*, July 21, 2013.

34. James Q. Wilson, "Crime," in *Beyond the Color Line: New Perspectives on Race and Ethnicity in America,* eds. Abigail Thernstrom and Stephan Thernstrom (Hoover Institution Press, 2002), 121, 123.

CHAPTER FOUR

1. Paul Moreno, "Unions and Discrimination," *Cato Journal* 30, no. 1 (Winter 2010), 69.

2. Ray Marshall, *The Negro Worker* (Random House, 1967), 63.

3. David Card and Alan B. Krueger, *Myth and Measurement: The New Economics of the Minimum Wage* (Princeton University Press, 1995), 4.

4. Gary S. Becker and Guity Nashat Becker, *The Economics of Life: From Baseball to Affirmative Action to Immigration, How Real-World Issues Affect Our Everyday Life* (McGraw-Hill, 1997), 37.

5. David Neumark and William L. Wascher, *Minimum Wages* (MIT Press, 2008), 104.

6. David Neumark, in discussion with the author, February 9, 2013.

7. Card and Krueger, *Myth and Measurement*, 236.

8. Neumark and Wascher, *Minimum Wages*, 65.

9. Bureau of the Census, http://www.census.gov/population /projections/data/national/2012/downloadablefiles.html.

10. Bureau of the Census, http://www.census.gov/prod/cen2010 /briefs/c2010br-06.pdf.

11. "The Racial Gap in College Student Graduation Rates," *Journal of Blacks in Higher Education*, October 19, 2012, http://www .jbhe.com/2012/10/the-racial-gap-in-college-student-graduation -rates-2/.

12. Rick Wartzman, "How Minimum Wage Lost Its Status As a Tool of Social Progress in the U.S.," *Wall Street Journal*, July 19, 2001.

13. Neumark and Wascher, *Minimum Wages*, 14.

14. Jim Powell, *FDR's Folly: How Roosevelt and His New Deal Prolonged the Great Depression* (Three Rivers Press, 2004), 118–19.

15. Morgan O. Reynolds, *Power and Privilege: Labor Unions in America* (Universe Books, 1984), 96.

16. Review & Outlook, "Look for the Union Label," *Wall Street Journal*, June 10, 2008.

17. Richard Vedder and Lowell Gallaway, "Declining Black Employment," *Society* 30, no. 5 (July–August 1993), 57.

18. Walter E. Williams, *Race and Economics: How Much Can Be Blamed on Discrimination?* (Hoover Institution Press, 2011), 34.

19. David E. Bernstein, *Only One Place of Redress: African Americans, Labor Regulations, and the Courts from Reconstruction to the New Deal* (Duke University Press, 2001), 74–77.

20. David R. Henderson, *The Joy of Freedom: An Economist's Odyssey* (Prentice Hall, 2002), 112–13.

21. Thomas Sowell, *Intellectuals and Society* (Basic Books, 2011), 450.

22. William E. Even and David A. Macpherson, "Unequal Harm: Racial Disparities in the Employment Consequences of Minimum Wage

Increases," Employment Policies Institute, May 5, 2011, http://www
.epionline.org/study/r137/.

23. *Statement of Robert B. Reich, Secretary of Labor, Before the Joint
Economic Committee,* February 22, 1995, (congressional testimony),
http://www.dol.gov/dol/aboutdol/history/reich/congress/022295rr
.htm.

24. Thomas Sowell, *Basic Economics: A Common Sense Guide to
the Economy* (Basic Books, 2007), 213.

CHAPTER FIVE

1. Andy Smarick, *The Urban School System of the Future: Applying
the Principles and Lessons of Chartering* (Rowman & Littlefield Education, 2012), 13.

2. National Center for Education Statistics, *Achievement Gaps:
How Black and White Students in Public Schools Perform in Mathematics and Reading on the National Assessment of Educational Progress,*
Department of Education, July 2009, http://nces.ed.gov/nations
reportcard/pubs/studies/2009455.aspx.

3. David Salisbury and Casey Lartigue Jr., eds., *Educational
Freedom in Urban America:* Brown v. Board *After Half a Century*
(Cato Institute, 2004), 115.

4. "Achievement Gap," *Education Week,* July 7, 2011, http://www
.edweek.org/ew/issues/achievement-gap/.

5. National Center for Education Statistics, *District Profiles,*
Department of Education, http://nces.ed.gov/nationsreportcard
/districts/.

6. Michael Winerip, "For Detroit Schools, Mixed Picture on
Reforms," *New York Times,* March 13, 2011.

7. David L. Kirp, "The Widest Achievement Gap," *National
Affairs* no. 5 (Fall 2010).

8. *The Urgency of Now: The Schott 50 State Report on Public Education and Black Males 2012*, Schott Foundation for Public Education, http://blackboysreport.org/urgency-of-now.

9. Andrew J. Coulson, "America Has Too Many Teachers," *Wall Street Journal*, July 10, 2012.

10. Paul E. Peterson, *Saving Schools: From Horace Mann to Virtual Learning* (Belknap Press, 2010), 11.

11. Cindy Johnston, "The Cost of Dropping Out," NPR, July 24, 2011, http://www.npr.org/2011/07/24/138508517/series-overview -the-cost-of-dropping-out.

12. Kirp, "The Widest Achievement Gap."

13. Christopher Jencks and Meredith Phillips, eds., *The Black-White Test Score Gap* (Brookings Institution Press, 1998), 6, 7.

14. Abigail Thernstrom and Stephan Thernstrom, *No Excuses: Closing the Racial Gap in Learning* (Simon & Schuster, 2003), 217, 218.

15. Trip Gabriel, "Despite Image, Union Leader Backs School Change," *New York Times*, October 15, 2010.

16. Terry M. Moe, "No Teacher Left Behind," *Wall Street Journal*, January 13, 2005.

17. Review & Outlook, "Teachers' Pets (Cont'd)," *Wall Street Journal*, January 27, 2006.

18. Nick Anderson, "Input of Teachers Unions Key to Successful Entries in Race to the Top," *Washington Post*, April 3, 2010.

19. James D. Anderson, *The Education of Blacks in the South, 1860–1935* (University of North Carolina Press, 1988), 4–18.

20. David Whitman, *Sweating the Small Stuff: Inner-City Schools and the New Paternalism* (Thomas B. Fordham Institute, 2008), 225.

21. Review & Outlook, "Witness Protection for Teachers," *Wall Street Journal*, November 24, 2003.

22. Steven Brill, *Class Warfare: Inside the Fight to Fix America's Schools* (Simon & Schuster, 2011), 16.

23. Ibid., 14.

24. Paul E. Peterson, "Charter Schools and Student Performance," *Wall Street Journal*, March 16, 2010.

25. Caroline M. Hoxby, Sonali Murarka, and Jenny Kang, *How New York City's Charter Schools Affect Achievement*, second report in a series, New York City Charter Schools Evaluation Project, September 2009.

26. Ron W. Zimmer and Cassandra M. Guarino, "Is There Empirical Evidence That Charter Schools 'Push Out' Low-Performing Students?" Education Evaluation and Policy Analysis, October 21, 2013, http://epa.sagepub.com/content/35/4/461.

27. Marcus A. Winters, *Why the Gap? Special Education and New York City Charter Schools*, Center on Reinventing Public Education, September 2013, http://www.crpe.org/publications/why-gap-special-education-and-new-york-city-charter-schools.

28. Jay P. Greene and Greg Forster, *Effects of Funding Incentives on Special Education Enrollment*, Civic Report no. 32 (December 2002), Manhattan Institute, http://www.manhattan-institute.org/html/cr_32.htm.

29. Brill, *Class Warfare*, 16.

30. Terry M. Moe, *Special Interests: Teachers Unions and America's Public Schools* (Brookings Institution Press, 2011), 266.

31. Sam Dillon, "Large Urban-Suburban Gap Seen in Graduation Rates," *New York Times*, April 22, 2009.

32. *The Value of Education Choices: Saving the D.C. Opportunity Scholarship Program, Hearing Before the Senate Committee on Homeland Security and Governmental Operations*, February 16, 2011 (written testimony of Dr. Patrick J. Wolf), http://*www.hsgac.senate.gov/download/2011-02-16-wolf-testimony* [download].

33. Matthew M. Chingos and Paul E. Peterson, "The Impact of School Vouchers on College Enrollment," *Education Next* 13, no. 3 (Summer 2013).

34. Greg Forster, *A Win-Win Solution: The Empirical Evidence on School Choice,* Friedman Foundation for Educational Choice, April 17, 2013, http://www.edchoice.org/Research/Reports/A-Win -Win-Solution—The-Empirical-Evidence-on-School-Choice.aspx.

35. Review & Outlook, "Democrats and Poor Kids," *Wall Street Journal,* April 6, 2009.

36. Caitlin Emma, "Louisiana: Vouchers Don't Hurt Desegregation," *Politico,* November 8, 2013, http://www.politico.com/story /2013/11/louisiana-school-voucher-program-desegregation-99585 .html.

37. Anna J. Egalite and Jonathan N. Mills, "The Louisiana Scholarship Program," *Education Next* 14, no. 1 (Winter 2014).

38. Sol Stern, *Breaking Free: Public School Lessons and the Imperative of School Choice,* (Encounter, 2003), 216.

39. Robert Balfanz, John M. Bridgeland, Mary Bruce, and Joanna Hornig Fox, *Building a Grad Nation: Progress and Challenge in Ending the High School Dropout Epidemic—Annual Update 2013,* a report by Civic Enterprises, the Everyone Graduates Center at Johns Hopkins University School of Education, America's Promise Alliance, and the Alliance for Excellent Education, February 2013, http://www .americaspromise.org/~/media/Files/Our%20Work/Grad%20 Nation/Building%20a%20Grad%20Nation/BuildingAGrad Nation2013Full.ashx.

40. Douglas Belkin and Cameron McWhirter, "Student-Loan Curbs Leave Black Schools in Peril," *Wall Street Journal,* October 2, 2013.

41. "Tracking Graduation Rates at HBCUs," *Journal of Blacks in Higher Education*, January 5, 2012, http://www.jbhe.com/2012/01/tracking-graduation-rates-at-hbcus/.

42. Roland G. Fryer and Michael Greenstone, "The Changing Consequences of Attending Historically Black Colleges and Universities," *American Economic Journal: Applied Economics* 2, no. 1 (January 2010), 118.

43. Ibid., 144.

44. Bill Maxwell, "The Once and Future Promise," *Tampa Bay Times*, May 27, 2007.

45. Cynthia Tucker, "Don't Waste Opportunity to Merge Black, White Colleges," *Atlanta Journal-Constitution*, December 10, 2008.

46. Adam Lynch, "Jackson State President: HBCUs' Future at Risk," *Jackson Free Press*, January 29, 2010.

47. Juan Williams, *Thurgood Marshall: American Revolutionary* (Times Books, 1998), 232.

CHAPTER SIX

1. Nathan Glazer, *Affirmative Discrimination* (Harvard University Press, 1987), xi.

2. Peter Kirsanow, "Government-Sponsored Discrimination Proliferates," *National Review Online*, May 31, 2011.

3. Randall Kennedy, *For Discrimination: Race, Affirmative Action, and the Law* (Pantheon, 2013), 18.

4. Sheryl Gay Stolberg and Dalia Sussman, "Gay Marriage Seen in Poll as Issue for the States," *New York Times*, June 7, 2013.

5. Stuart Taylor, "Do African-Americans Really Want Racial Preferences?" *National Journal*, December 20, 2002.

6. Glazer, *Discrimination*, viii.

7. Adam Liptak, "Justices Step Up Scrutiny of Race in College Entry," *New York Times*, June 25, 2013.

8. Russell K. Nieli, *Wounds That Will Not Heal: Affirmative Action and Our Continuing Racial Divide* (Encounter, 2012), 383–84.

9. Stephan Thernstrom and Abigail Thernstrom, *America in Black and White: One Nation, Indivisible* (Simon & Schuster, 1997), 186–87.

10. Jennifer L. Hochschild, *Facing Up to the American Dream: Race, Class, and the Soul of the Nation* (Princeton University Press, 1996), 48.

11. Sean F. Reardon and Kendra Bischoff, *Growth in the Residential Segregation of Families by Income, 1970–2009*, Russell Sage Foundation, November 2011, http://www.scribd.com/doc/72915429/Growth -in-the-Residential-Segregation-of-Families-by-Income-1970-2009.

12. Richard Arum and Josipa Roksa, *Academically Adrift: Limited Learning on College Campuses* (University of Chicago Press, 2011), 46–47.

13. Thernstrom and Thernstrom, *Black and White*, 398–400.

14. Nieli, *Wounds*, 106–07.

15. *Black First-Year Students at the Nation's Leading Research Universities*, JBHE Annual Survey 2012, *Journal of Blacks in Higher Education*, December 2011, http://www.jbhe.com/2011/12 /jbhe-annual-survey-black-first-year-students-at-the-nations-leading -research-universities/.

16. Michael A. Fletcher, "Wider Fallout Seen From Race-Neutral Admissions," *Washington Post*, April 19, 2003.

17. Richard Pérez-Peña, "In California, Push for College Diversity Starts Earlier," *New York Times*, May 7, 2013.

18. Richard H. Sander and Stuart Taylor Jr., *Mismatch: How Affirmative Action Hurts Students It's Intended to Help, and Why Universities Won't Admit It* (Basic Books, 2012), 154.

19. Brief for Gail Heriot, Peter Kirsanow, and Todd Gaziano, members of the U.S. Commission on Civil Rights, in Support of the

Petitioner, Fisher v. University of Texas, No. 11-345 (2012), http://www
.americanbar.org/publications/preview_home/11-345.html.

20. Heather Mac Donald, "Affirmative Disaster," *Weekly Standard*,
February 20, 2012.

21. Sander and Taylor, *Mismatch*, 4.

22. Stephan Thernstrom and Abigail Thernstrom, "Reflections
on *The Shape of the River*," *UCLA Law Review* 46 (June 1999),
1610–11.

23. Kennedy, *Discrimination*, 9–10.

24. William O. Douglas, *The Court Years, 1939–1975: The Autobiography of William O. Douglas* (Vintage Books, 1981), 149.

25. Stephen L. Carter, *Reflections of an Affirmative Action Baby*
(Basic Books, 1991), 15–16.

26. Thomas, *A Memoir*, 142.

27. Ibid., 87.

28. Noah Bierman and Frank Phillips, "Bad Week May Haunt
Warren," *Boston Globe*, May 5, 2012.

29. Scott Jaschik, "Asians and Affirmative Action," *Inside Higher
Ed*, May 30, 2012, http://www.insidehighered.com/news/2012
/05/30/asian-american-group-urges-supreme-court-bar-race
-conscious-admissions.

30. Ibid.

INDEX